D0771035

FRANKIE AVALON'S
Italian Family Cookbook

WITHDRAWN

FRANKIE AVALON'S
Italian Family Cookbook

FROM MOM'S KITCHEN
TO MINE AND YOURS

FRANKIE AVALON

with RICK RODGERS

ST. MARTIN'S GRIFFIN
NEW YORK

FRANKIE AVALON'S ITALIAN FAMILY COOKBOOK. Copyright © 2015 by
Frankie Avalon. All rights reserved. Printed in China.
For information, address St. Martin's Press,
175 Fifth Avenue, New York, N.Y. 10010.

Designed by Jan Derevjanik

www.stmartins.com

The Library of Congress Cataloging-in-Publication Data is available upon request.

ISBN 978-1-250-05913-0 (paper over board)
ISBN 978-1-4668-6371-2 (e-book)

Photographs on pp. ii, iv, viii, 3, 15, 33, 36-37, 57, 60-61, 65,
125, 134, 141, and 184-185 by Teri Lyn Fisher.

Food photographs and photographs on pp. 4, 6-7, 9, 10, 13, 16, 18-19,
34, 58, 70-71, 74, 91, 94, 97-98, 100-101, 111, 116, 121, 137, 140,
157-158, 160-161, 181-182, 188-189, 201, and 208 by Ellen Silverman.

St. Martin's Griffin books may be purchased for educational, business,
or promotional use. For information on bulk purchases, please contact
the Macmillan Corporate and Premium Sales Department at 1-800-
221-7945, extension 5442, or write to specialmarkets@macmillan.com.

First Edition: September 2015

10 9 8 7 6 5 4 3 2 1

THIS BOOK IS DEDICATED TO
Keith Frankel and John Peca

contents

introduction

As a performer, I find myself away from home a lot, as being on the road is a big part of the job. I'm used to it, though, because I've been in show business since high school. Whenever the grind of travel gets me down, I have a surefire way to keep me going: The knowledge that I will soon be returning to my home and family.

One of the greatest comforts of home life for me is home cooking—a kitchen filled with the aromas of simmering tomato "gravy," freshly chopped basil, and dessert baking in the oven is a beautiful and welcoming place. Every Sunday, I put on an apron, head to the

kitchen, and make a huge meal for my large family. How large is large? Well, I have been married to Kay for over fifty years, and we have eight great kids (Frank Junior, Tony, Dina, Laura, Joe, Nick, Kathryn, and Carla) born in a ten-year period. They, in turn, have given us ten wonderful grandchildren: Jonathan, Patrick, Kathryn, Connor, Nicole, Meghan, Mason, Bridget, Johnny, and Tucker). And what do I cook? What any good son of South Philadelphia would cook, of course—the zesty, traditional dishes of Italy.

Tradition is the key to our Sunday meals. Sunday dinners are a part of most Italian Americans' DNA—the day of the week set aside for family and friends to gather, relax, and create memories. Most of the time, the recipes I cook have been in our family for generations. Dad was a butcher, and for a time, we lived above the shop. How people put food on the table was a big part of our daily life. (The recipe for the sausage I sell through my food company is his recipe.) My mom worked, too, in the garment industry. Regardless, we had a

home-cooked meal on the table every night. When I hear people say that they are too busy to make dinner, I question it. All those years ago, the Avallones could not have been busier, but we cooked our meals from scratch.

I honor my mom and dad with my cooking, sharing their recipes and what they taught me about food, just as they shared knowledge from their parents with me. We never wasted food. Stale bread was turned into bread crumbs to use in other dishes, and last night's roast chicken carcass was simmered into a broth for soup, maybe made richer with some cheese custards floating in the broth. My sister Theresa is the guardian of my mom's recipe notebook, and many of these dishes come directly from those gravy-splattered pages. Now with this book, my family will always have my recipes for their favorites to pass down to their kids, continuing the thread of family history. They all love my crab marinara, tomato and onion salad, and banana icebox cake. (Speaking of iceboxes and family history, I won our family's first refrigerator at a talent contest when I was barely in my teens, proving to me that maybe I could make a living at this showbiz thing.)

With *Frankie Avalon's Italian Family Cookbook*, I can share these beloved recipes with you, too. For those of you who are of Italian extraction, these dishes are sure to bring back memories of your family meals, as many are classics that have been passed down from generation to generation. I am thinking of such specialties as stuffed calamari braised in marinara sauce, honey-dipped struffoli, and a big pot of meat-filled "Sunday gravy" that takes hours of simmering before it is ready to serve with a huge platter of pasta. I've put together the dishes that my family asks for again and again. I have also included recipes from a few of my favorite restaurants that remind me of meals at important times in my life, such as my favorite chili and the fettuccine Alfredo that Kay and I had on our honeymoon.

My life has been about extended family, too. Maybe you've seen me perform with Bobby Rydell, Fabian, or James Darren—guys I have known since I was a teenager. When researching this book, I went back to my old neighborhood in South Philadelphia, which was not only where most Italians settled, but the birthplace of an entire genre of singing personified by the friends I just mentioned and yours truly. I asked my buddy, Jerry Blavat, who has been a part of the Philly music scene since our days at *American Bandstand*, to join me, and you'll see some pictures of us together at our favorite haunts—Talluto's Authentic Italian Food, Isgro Pastries, Claudio's Specialty Foods, Cappuccio's Meats, and Darigo's Fish Market.

Frankie Avalon's Italian Family Cookbook is a simple title, but it tells it all. It is one thing to have a great restaurant meal, and I like them as much as the next person. But, making a delicious meal at home for loved family and friends, and basking in their presence and the memories of the ones who may not be at the table—I'll take that any day of the week.

—Frankie Avalon

the avalon family kitchen

Both my parents worked, but we had a hot meal on the table every night because they were always prepared with ingredients in the pantry and fridge. Dad would usually bring a cut of meat or a chicken home from the butcher shop, but you can do almost the same thing with a quick stop at the store to purchase a bit of fresh meat, seafood, or poultry. The key is to stock the kitchen with a few well-chosen staples to complete the meal. How many times have I returned from the road thinking that I have nothing in the house to eat for dinner? And then . . . I boil a bowlful of pasta, toss it with some garlic cooked in olive oil, and finish it with a generous grating of Romano or a dollop of ricotta.

In Italy, each region has its own specialties, dishes that don't travel far outside of its boundaries. To this day, some Italians divide the country and its cuisine in half: by north of Rome and the regions south of it (including Sicily). An Italian would consider Parmesan a Northern cheese, and Romano a Southern one, whereas it's all just Italian cheese to an American cook! So, because my family is from the south, my recipes tend to use tomatoes, Romano, oregano, garlic, and other foods that are synonymous with that area's cooking.

If you are of Italian heritage, then you probably already know a market that sells Italian specialties. Many, if not all, of the groceries listed below are available in supermarkets and specialty stores. Most American cities and towns with citizens of Italian heritage have "dairy stores" (*latticini*) specializing in freshly made ricotta, hand-pulled mozzarella, and imported cheeses. Or you might have a cheese shop, specialty food store, or delicatessen that carries these delicacies and staples.

Here are the Italian American cooking essentials that I keep on hand in my kitchen:

CHEESE

Italy has countless cheeses, but there are five that I use over and over. You might also call them cooking (as opposed to eating) cheeses.

GRATING CHEESES
These hard, aged cheeses are grated and added to food to provide a sharp flavor.

Pecorino Romano • My go-to grating cheese is made from sheep's milk, and hails from the area around Rome. This cheese is sharper than Parmesan, and it is a better match for the spicy foods that I love. Buy chunks of Pecorino

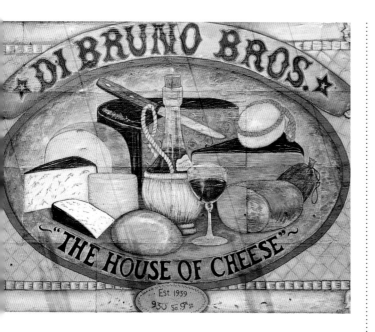

even exist. For simplicity's sake, in this book, I call Parmigiano-Reggiano by its common name, Parmesan. Grate and store it like Romano.

FRESH CHEESES

These soft cheeses are best bought in small batches. They have a relatively short storage life, although the factory-produced versions last longer.

Mozzarella • We are all familiar with mass-produced mozzarella, which is easily purchased at the supermarket. But more and more good cooks are getting to know creamy fresh mozzarella. To make it, cow's (or sometimes water buffalo's) milk is heated until it solidifies into a soft curd, and this mass is stretched and shaped by hand into balls or logs. It is very popular as a melting cheese. Fresh mozzarella is too soft to shred, and it should be cut into small cubes before cooking. If you really want to shred it (old habits die hard), freeze the mozzarella for an hour or two until it firms up. Fresh mozzarella is often sold packed in brine, and can only be kept refrigerated for a few days after purchase.

Ricotta • In Sicily, this spreadable cheese with tiny curds is made from sheep's milk, but in America, cow's milk is the main ingredient. I love fresh ricotta, which can be found at many Italian grocers and cheese stores. While supermarket-style ricotta can be made with part-skim milk, fresh ricotta is always made from whole milk, and has an unsurpassed rich flavor and moist texture. In fact, fresh ricotta is usually drained before using to remove excess liquid. Just put the ricotta in a paper towel–lined wire sieve suspended over a bowl, making sure that the bottom of the sieve is at least 3 inches above the bottom of the bowl. Let stand at room temperature until some whey has

Romano (also known by its common name, Romano), and for the freshest flavor, grate it just before using because pregrated Romano loses its moisture and flavor quickly. Wrapped in plastic, the chunk will keep for about a month in the refrigerator. The name pecorino may also refer to several eating cheeses made all over Italy, so be sure that you get Pecorino Romano (Locatelli is a reliable brand) if you intend to use it for cooking.

Parmigiano-Reggiano • While I personally prefer Pecorino Romano, many cooks consider Parmesan to be the ultimate grating cheese. Its mellow, nutty flavor is very versatile, but I like to reserve it for delicate foods and creamy sauces. For my everyday cooking, give me Romano. While you can buy Parmesan made in the United States, or even Chile, it cannot hold a candle to the real thing, which is made from cow's milk in the area around Parma, Italy. Look for imported Italian Parmigiano-Reggiano, with the name stamped in continuous script on its golden rind. Pass over the domestic Parmesan, and just pretend like the stuff in the can doesn't

drained into the bowl, about 4 or 5 tablespoons for a pound of cheese. If the kitchen is warm, refrigerate the draining setup.

SEMISOFT CHEESE

With a texture that is just firm enough to grate, this category of cheese is usually sliced and eaten as antipasti or after dinner.

Fontina Val d'Aosta • A specialty of the Aosta Valley in the Italian Alps, this wonderful cheese with an earthy aroma has been made since the twelfth century. Other countries make copycats of the original, with such derivative names as Fontinella or Fontal, but they are much milder. Young Fontina Val d'Aosta is creamy with a tan rind, but aging can make the cheese firmer and the rind darker. The real beauty of Fontina shows when it is melted, as it is smooth without the stringiness of melted mozzarella.

BREAD CRUMBS

Could there be a duller subject than bread crumbs? Actually, it is a very important ingredient in the Italian American kitchen, and there is quite a distinction between the soft and dried versions, which are used as to coat, bind, and even flavor foods.

SOFT BREAD CRUMBS

Soft bread crumbs are made from slightly stale (not hard) bread, and are sometimes referred to as fresh to distinguish them from the dried store-bought variety. Back before carb-counting was in (which is done even in my pasta-loving family), every Italian family served crusty bread with each meal. This much fresh bread

inevitably led to stale bread, which can be processed into crumbs. These days, even if you don't have a lot of bread in your house, you can buy an Italian roll or two specifically to prepare fresh bread crumbs.

To make fresh bread crumbs, cut the bread, crust and all, into 2- to 3-inch pieces. Working in batches, toss the bread into a food processor and process it into coarse crumbs. This will take longer than you might expect, at least a minute or two. (If using a blender. process the bread in somewhat small batches to make about ½ cup of crumbs at a time.) Bread crumbs can be stored in a zippered plastic storage bag in the freezer for up to 3 months. They don't need to be thawed before using. The crumbs are almost always soaked with liquid (usually milk) to soften before mixing with other ingredients.

DRIED BREAD CRUMBS

Dried bread crumbs are sold in three varieties: plain, Italian-seasoned, and Italian-seasoned with Romano cheese. Stored in a cool, dry place, they have a long shelf life. They are much finer than the soft, fresh crumbs, so they are often used as a coating for food or as a binder for meatballs.

TOMATOES

In music, it is difficult to make an impression with a bad song. In Southern Italian cooking, you need great canned tomatoes. It's that simple. In Italy, the growing season is long, so they can cook with sweet, vine-ripened tomatoes. We don't have that advantage all over our country, but, luckily, there are a lot of good tomatoes available.

The most famous tomato, canned or otherwise, is the San Marzano plum variety, grown in the volcanic soil around Mount Vesuvius. I want to put one myth to rest right now: You do not need expensive imported

Working over a sieve set over a bowl, poke a hole in each tomato and shake out the seeds before hand-crushing them. Discard the seeds in the sieve, but add the juice in the bowl to the tomatoes.

SEASONINGS

Take away my bottle of dried oregano, and my cooking would suffer. I grew up with its pungent flavor and aroma, and to me, it personifies good home-style Italian cooking. Drying concentrates the oregano's oils, and fresh oregano just doesn't have the same intense flavor.

That doesn't mean that I don't cook with fresh herbs—oregano is the exception, not the rule. Herbs are the leaves of aromatic edible plants used to flavor food. Their oils begin to dissipate right after chopping, so fresh herbs give a stronger, fresher flavor to foods. Parsley (the flat-leaf, Italian variety), thyme, rosemary, basil, and sage are always better fresh than dried. But if you can substitute the dried, whole leaf (not ground) version, I list it as an option in the ingredients list.

Because fresh herbs can be pricey, it is economical to grow them at home, either on a windowsill or in a garden. Store them, loosely wrapped in paper towels, in the refrigerator drawer. Fresh basil stores best with the stems in a glass of water, like a bouquet, covered loosely with a plastic bag in the refrigerator.

To chop fresh herbs, rinse them well and dry completely on paper towels or in a salad spinner. Pluck the leaves from the stems, chop the leaves with a large, very sharp knife, and use immediately. Only chop as much as you need for the dish you are cooking.

In some recipes, I use granulated garlic, which is a slightly coarser version of garlic powder, which can be substituted. This ingredient gives garlic flavor without its lumpy texture.

canned tomatoes to make top-notch Italian food. I cook all the time with excellent New Jersey or California tomatoes. (My sister even has a project selling canned Jersey tomatoes with the profits going to Eden Institute's Autism Services. Look for Avallone Crushed Tomatoes—our family named brand—at supermarkets in the Philadelphia area.) Once you find a brand that you like, stick with it. Canned tomatoes should have a bright red color and vibrant flavor. Skip the flavored ones as you can certainly add your own garlic and herbs.

I use crushed tomatoes most often because I like the thick body they give to sauces. In some recipes where I want a chunkier texture, I also use whole tomatoes in juice, drained, crushed, and the juices reserved. To do this, just pour the contents of the can, juices and all, into a large bowl. Reach into the bowl and squeeze the tomatoes between your fingers until they are coarsely crushed. You can also do this in a food processor, but drain the tomatoes first because the canning liquid tends to seep through the center shaft. I rarely remove the tomato seeds, but you can do so if you wish:

SPICES

Spices are the seeds, stems, bark, nut, or roots of a plant used for flavoring. Like herbs, these are best freshly ground, but some of these are too hard (cinnamon and cloves, for example) to grind easily at home. In this case, pepper is the exception, and it should always be freshly ground in a pepper mill. Store all spices and dried herbs in a cool, dark place away from the stove.

KOSHER SALT

This type of salt has a flaky texture that you can see when you sprinkle it on food. For that reason alone, many chefs prefer it to finely granulated table salt. Kosher salt also has a cleaner flavor because it doesn't have any additives like flowing agents. I also like the Himalayan pink salt that my buddy Sylvester Stallone gave me as a gift for seasoning salads and other foods after cooking. I do use fine table salt (either iodized or plain) in baking because it dissolves better than coarse salt.

I give a measurement for salt and pepper with raw foods like chicken and meat where you can't actually taste the food to determine how seasoning is needed. If you are using table salt, keep in mind that its small grains fill the measuring spoon more compactly, so for recipes where you can taste the food, I use the term "season to taste," so add as much salt and pepper as you like.

MEAT

You have probably heard the saying that farmers use every part of the pig except the oink. Two of the most flavorful pork products on the planet are Italian.

PROSCIUTTO

Prosciutto is basically Italian ham, but the leg is salted and cured to give the meat a firm texture. If it is to be used for an antipasto (melon and prosciutto is a classic), it is cut at the delicatessen into very thin slices. For cooking, ask the delicatessen staff to cut it slightly thicker, about the thickness of a playing card. (That is still thin, but not paper thin.)

PANCETTA

Pancetta is Italian bacon, from the pork belly, which is cured, but not smoked. It is rolled up into a cylinder. While it is fully cooked and can be sliced and eaten as is, pancetta is usually cooked to render its fat and flavor a dish.

Both prosciutto and pancetta are sold diced and packaged in very convenient packages. Look for these in the presliced cold cuts section of the market, or perhaps near the fresh pasta products.

BEEF AND VEAL

Ground veal is used much more than beef in traditional Italian cooking. There's a historical reason for this. Cattle are very big animals, and take a lot of feed to grow to maturity. There just isn't a lot of flat grazing ground in Italy, especially in the southern parts of the country, and mature cattle were more prized for milk than meat. So, the smaller calves provided the meat, which has a much more delicate flavor than ground beef, and it is naturally lean.

Here, in America, your supermarket may not carry ground veal as a matter of course unless it caters to an Italian American clientele. You can special order ground veal, or process it at home in a food processor. To do this, partially freeze 1-inch cubes of boneless veal shoulder for about an hour. Working in batches of about 8 ounces each, pulse the veal until it is very finely chopped.

If you wish, you can use ground round (15 percent fat) beef in these recipes, or use half beef and half veal. Or, you can even substitute ground turkey (but not the ground turkey breast, which is too lean). Veal, however, is my favorite for these dishes.

OLIVE OIL

Most olive oil—the cooking fat pressed out of olives—in this country actually comes from Spain. If you are an Italian American and want to remain true to the country of your ancestors, look carefully at the oil label to be sure it is a product of Italy, and not just imported from there.

Choose olive oil based on its flavor and viscosity. Some taste stronger than others. That can be a good thing for dipping bread, but not so great for cooking. And some oils can be quite thick and heavy. It is really best to have both of the major kinds of olive oil in your kitchen.

Extra-virgin olive oil, made from the first pressing of the olives, has a fresh, green tint and should have a distinctive taste. Depending on where the oil is from, it can taste vegetal, fruity, spicy, or grassy. I can't tell you what tastes good to you, so when you find one that you like, stick with it. Extra-virgin oil loses flavor when heated, so it is best to use it raw in salads or as a condiment to drizzle over foods.

If a recipe just calls for olive oil, I mean the standard golden type. This used to be called "pure" olive oil, which I guess was changed because someone thought that meant there was "un-pure" olive oil for sale, too. Anyway, this is a good oil for everyday cooking and for salads where you might not want a strong olive flavor.

WINE

There is a good reason why Italian cooking uses so much wine. Well, of course, the country's terrain and climate is perfect for growing a large variety of wine grapes, and cooks will use what they have on hand. But wine's big talent is how its alcohol brings out the flavors of the other ingredients while providing a taste of its own. Always use a tasty wine fit for drinking, and never the supermarket "cooking wine," which is made from very inferior wine and heavily salted.

When purchasing a red cooking wine, look for a reasonably priced, full-bodied Italian Chianti. Don't get anything too expensive because wines that have been aged in oak can transfer the wood flavor to the food. California Shiraz is a good substitute. Pinot Grigio is a fine choice for a white cooking wine.

VERMOUTH AND SHERRY

When I was growing up in South Philly, fortified wine, such as sherry or vermouth (both sweet and dry), was more common than drinking wine. Every family had a bottle or two in the house for "medicinal purposes," or to serve before dinner, or after dinner with cookies. (Everyone knows that cookies are even better dunked in wine, right?) Vermouth and sherry were originally "fortified" with additional alcohol so they stored well during long shipping around the world. At home, fortified wines kept longer without refrigeration than the drinking wine that needed to be refrigerated after opening, a distinct advantage. These days, when unfortified wine is more common, I just use them for their flavor.

Vermouth is wine that has been flavored with herbs and spices. Dry vermouth, made from white wine, can stand in for white wine in cooking. Don't confuse it with bianco, another vermouth type. Sweetened red wine is the base for sweet (or red) vermouth, although it is not a substitute for Chianti in recipes. You can use either an imported European or a top-quality California brand.

Dry sherry (sometimes labeled fino) is a really useful cooking wine, with a slightly nutty and not too sweet flavor. While sherry is originally from Spain (Tio Pepe Fino is a good choice), a less expensive California brand is fine. Other sherry types, such as amontillado or manzanillo, are too sweet and heavy for cooking.

Veal Chops   T.Bone/Porterhouse

antipasti

BRUSCHETTA WITH BELL PEPPERS, OLIVES, AND BASIL 20

SALAMI-STUFFED MUSHROOMS 23

STUFFED ARTICHOKES 24

GRILLED TOMATO CAPRESE 25

RICE BALLS 26

STUFFED EGGS WITH MASCARPONE, BASIL,
AND PANCETTA 29

SWEET-AND-SOUR VEGETABLES 30

CLAMS OREGANATA 31

Broccoli
$ 200
2

String
Beans
3 pounds
$4
$1.50 per pound

bruschetta
with bell peppers, olives, and basil

MAKES 24; 6 TO 8 SERVINGS

When you need to serve a crowd without a lot of effort, bruschetta is the way to go—it's just toasted bread with topping. But with a great topping, it gets a party off on the right foot. This light but flavorful vegetable topping is good for when you know you have a big meat or pasta main course on the menu. My method for skinning the peppers cuts them into long strips so they are easier to cook without a lot of turning. For the toasts, use bread that is long and relatively thin so you have just a bite or two per bruschetta.

3 large bell peppers

2 tablespoons red wine vinegar

½ teaspoon hot red pepper flakes

1 garlic clove, minced

2 tablespoons extra-virgin olive oil

½ cup coarsely chopped pitted kalamata olives

2 tablespoons finely chopped fresh basil

2 tablespoons drained nonpareil capers (optional)

Kosher salt and freshly ground black pepper

24 slices crusty bread, cut from a long, narrow loaf, such as a ficelle

Extra-virgin olive oil, for brushing

1. Prepare an outdoor grill for direct cooking over high heat. (Or position a broiler rack about 6 inches from the heat source and preheat the broiler.)

2. Cut the top and bottom end off each bell pepper, discarding the stem. Make a vertical cut into each pepper and open it up into a long strip. Trim away and discard the ribs and seeds. Grill the peppers, skin side down, with the lid closed as much as possible, until the skins have blackened, 6 to 8 minutes. (Or broil the peppers, skin side up, until the skins have blackened and blistered, 6 to 8 minutes.) Transfer to a bowl, cover with a plate, and let cool for about 10 minutes.

3. Meanwhile, brush the bread slices on both sides with the oil. Grill, turning as needed, until toasted, 1 to 2 minutes. Transfer the toasts to a platter. (The toasts can be cooled, covered, and stored at room temperature for up to 8 hours.)

4. Whisk the vinegar, red pepper flakes, and garlic together in a medium bowl. Gradually whisk in the oil. Peel the bell peppers, cut them into ½-inch dice, and stir into the bowl with the oil. Add the olives, basil, and capers, if using, and mix well. Season to taste with salt and black pepper. Cover and marinate at room temperature for at least 1 or up to 4 hours.

5. To serve, top each toast with the bell pepper mixture and serve immediately.

salami-stuffed mushrooms

MAKES 16; 6 TO 8 SERVINGS

It's easy to say that everyone loves stuffed mushrooms. Knowing this, I served these recently to my family, and they disappeared from the platter in just a few minutes. Use the extra-large "gourmet" or "stuffing" mushrooms because they will shrink during cooking. I only recommend Genoa salami as a generic suggestion; you can use any kind of salami that you like.

....

16 large "gourmet" or "stuffing" mushrooms (about 28 ounces)

4 tablespoons olive oil, plus more for drizzling

Kosher salt and freshly ground black pepper

½ cup finely chopped Genoa salami (2 ounces)

¼ cup finely chopped yellow onion

1 garlic clove, minced

1 cup Italian-seasoned dried bread crumbs

¼ cup freshly grated Pecorino Romano cheese (1 ounce)

1 tablespoon finely chopped fresh flat-leaf parsley

2 large eggs, beaten

1. Remove the stems from the mushrooms, keeping the caps intact, and reserving the stems. Transfer the caps to a large bowl, drizzle with 3 tablespoons of the oil, and toss to coat them with the oil.

2. Pulse the reserved stems in a food processor until finely chopped (or use a large knife). Heat the remaining 1 tablespoon oil in a large skillet over medium heat. Add the chopped stems and season them lightly with ¼ teaspoon salt and ⅛ teaspoon pepper. Cook, stirring occasionally, until they give off their juices and begin to brown. Add the salami, onion, and garlic and cook, stirring often, until the onion has softened, about 2 minutes. Transfer the stem mixture to a medium bowl and cool slightly.

3. Stir in the bread crumbs, Romano, and parsley. Season to taste with salt and pepper. Stir in the eggs.

4. Lightly oil a 9 by 13-inch baking dish. Arrange the caps, stemmed side up, in the dish and season them with ½ teaspoon salt and ½ teaspoon pepper. Using a dessertspoon, stuff each cap with the bread crumb mixture, pressing it firmly into a mound. (The mushrooms can be covered with plastic wrap and refrigerated for up to 4 hours.)

5. Position a rack in the upper third of the oven and preheat the oven to 375°F.

6. Drizzle the mushrooms with oil. Bake until the topping is lightly browned, about 20 minutes. Let cool slightly and serve warm.

stuffed artichokes
with romano and garlic

MAKES 4 SERVINGS

If you want to bring a smile to my face, put a stuffed artichoke on the table in front of me. They aren't difficult to make, but they always take time to cook. Boiled, then stuffed with bread crumbs and baked, these are a fine first course to a special dinner, or serve them for a light lunch. One thing peculiar about artichokes is that they contain a rare chemical (cynarin) that makes wine taste sweet, so keep that in mind when choosing a beverage.

4 medium artichokes, about 9 ounces each

1 lemon, halved, plus lemon quarters, for serving

STUFFING

3½ cups fresh bread crumbs, made from day-old bread

1¼ cups freshly grated Pecorino Romano cheese (5 ounces)

3 tablespoons minced fresh flat-leaf parsley

3 garlic cloves, minced

¼ cup extra-virgin olive oil, plus more for the baking dish and drizzling

Kosher salt and freshly ground black pepper

1. Bring a large pot of salted water to a boil over high heat. Cut off the top ½ inch from each artichoke. Using kitchen scissors, snip the thorny tips from the leaves. Rub the cut parts of the artichoke with a lemon half.

2. Add the artichokes to the pot and cover tightly. Reduce the heat to low and cook at a steady, low boil until an artichoke leaf can be easily pulled off, 45 minutes to 1 hour. Drain the artichokes in a large colander. Turn the artichokes upside down and let drain and cool completely.

3. To make the stuffing: Mix the bread crumbs, Romano, parsley, and garlic together in a medium bowl. Stir in enough of the oil to moisten the crumbs. Season to taste with salt and pepper.

4. Position a rack in the center of the oven and preheat the oven to 375°F. Lightly oil a 9 by 13-inch baking dish.

5. Working with each artichoke one at a time, hold it upside down and squeeze it gently but firmly to extrude excess water, making sure to keep the artichoke intact. Force about one-quarter of the bread crumb mixture between the outer artichoke leaves (don't bother with the thin leaves in the center of the artichoke). Place the stuffed artichoke in the baking dish.

6. Drizzle olive oil over the artichokes. Bake, uncovered, until the stuffing is lightly browned, about 30 minutes. Let cool for 10 minutes. Serve warm or cooled to room temperature, with the lemon wedges.

grilled tomato caprese
with pesto

MAKES 6 SERVINGS

Tomato Salad Caprese (from the isle of Capri), is classically made with ripe tomatoes, fresh mozzarella, and beautiful fresh basil leaves—it is never served with vinegar, balsamic or otherwise. Here's a variation with grilled tomatoes which is equally delicious, as the heat softens the cheese, and the pesto brings a few more flavors than basil leaves alone. Serve this with crusty bread or focaccia.

9 ripe plum tomatoes, halved lengthwise

Extra-virgin olive oil

¾ cup Pesto (page 87)

1 pound fresh mozzarella cheese, cut into 12 equal pieces

Kosher salt and freshly ground black pepper

1. Prepare an outdoor grill for direct cooking over medium-high heat (450° to 500°F).

2. Lightly brush the tomatoes all over with a tablespoon or two of the oil. Brush the grill grates clean. Place the tomatoes, skin side down, on the grill. Grill, with the lid closed as much as possible, until the skins are seared with grill marks, about 3 minutes. Flip the tomatoes and cook, cut sides down, with the lid closed, until the other sides are seared with grill marks, 1 to 2 minutes more. Using a metal spatula, transfer the tomatoes to a platter.

3. For each serving, spread about 1½ tablespoons of the pesto in a pool in the center of each plate. Alternate 3 tomato halves with 2 mozzarella pieces on each plate. Season to taste with salt and pepper and serve.

Antipasti • 25

rice balls

MAKES ABOUT 15

One of the most popular of all Italian appetizers, these fried balls are sometimes called *arancini* ("oranges") because of their shape and color. With a crispy coating and creamy rice interior, they can be served plain with a squeeze of lemon, or in a pool of marinara or Bolognese sauce. The important thing is that you make them! To shape the balls, a food portion scoop works better than pressing the rice mixture into balls with your hands alone.

RICE FILLING

1 cup Arborio rice

2 cups water

1½ teaspoons kosher salt

½ cup shredded Fontina Val d'Aosta cheese

2 large eggs, beaten

2 tablespoons plain dried bread crumbs

1 tablespoon finely chopped fresh flat-leaf parsley

½ teaspoon freshly ground black pepper

1½ cups plain dried bread crumbs, for coating

Vegetable oil, for deep-frying

note: You will find the perfect food portion scoop at restaurant supply shops and online. These scoops are standardized by a color-coded handle and by number. I use a red-handle #24 scoop, with a 2-inch diameter that holds about 2½ tablespoons.

1. To prepare the rice filling: Bring the rice, water, and ½ teaspoon of the salt to a boil in a medium saucepan over medium heat. Reduce the heat to low and tightly cover the saucepan. Cook until the rice is tender and has absorbed the water, about 20 minutes. Remove from the heat and let stand, covered, for 5 minutes.

2. Transfer the rice to a medium bowl and let cool completely. Stir in the Fontina, eggs, bread crumbs, parsley, the remaining 1 teaspoon salt, and the pepper. Cover and refrigerate for at least 15 minutes and up to 1 hour.

3. Line a baking sheet with parchment or wax paper. To make each ball, using a 3-ounce spring-loaded food portion scoop (see Note) dipped in cold water, scoop up the rice mixture, press it firmly in the scoop to mold it into a ball with one flat side, and release it onto the baking sheet. Using wet hands rinsed under cold water, shape each into a round ball. (The balls can be refrigerated for up to 2 hours. Let stand at room temperature for 15 minutes before frying.)

4. Position a rack in the center of the oven and preheat the oven to 200°F. Line another baking sheet with brown paper (from a grocery bag) or paper towels. Pour enough oil into a deep saucepan to come 3 inches up the sides and heat over high heat until it reaches 350°F on a deep-frying thermometer.

5. Spread the bread crumbs in a shallow dish. One at a time, roll the rice balls in the bread crumbs to coat them, patting the crumbs to help them adhere. Return the balls to the wax paper–lined baking sheet. Working in batches without crowding, add the balls to the oil and deep-fry until golden brown, about 3 minutes. Using a wire spider or slotted spoon, transfer the balls to the brown paper–lined baking sheet and keep warm in the oven while frying the rest. Serve hot.

stuffed eggs
with mascarpone, basil, and pancetta

MAKES 4 TO 6 SERVINGS

Stuffed eggs fit into the American appetizer category more easily than Italian antipasti, but this recipe with Mediterranean flavors mixes the best of both worlds. No one likes overcooked hard-boiled eggs with that strange green color to the yolks, but my low-heat method avoids this problem. Also, I always cook a couple of extra eggs to be sure to make enough filling.

8 large eggs

3 tablespoons mascarpone cheese

1 slice pancetta, cooked until crisp, finely chopped

2 tablespoons minced fresh basil, plus more for garnish

Kosher salt and freshly ground black pepper

1. Place the eggs in a large saucepan and add enough cold water to cover. Bring just to a strong simmer over high heat. Remove the saucepan from the heat and cover tightly. Let stand for 20 minutes.

2. Meanwhile, cook the pancetta in a small skillet over medium heat, turning occasionally, until crisped and browned, about 5 minutes. Transfer to paper towels and let cool. Finely chop the pancetta, cover, and refrigerate until serving time.

3. Using a slotted spoon, transfer the eggs to a bowl of ice water. Let the eggs stand until chilled, about 10 minutes. Crack the eggs. Starting at the largest end, and working under a thin stream of cold running water, remove the egg shells.

4. Cut each egg in half lengthwise and remove the yolks. Discard four of the cooked egg white halves or save them for another use. Using a rubber spatula, rub the yolks through a fine sieve into a small bowl. Stir in the mascarpone and basil and season to taste with salt and pepper. Dividing it equally, spoon the filling into the whites. (For a more professional look, transfer the yolk mixture to a pastry bag fitted with a ½-inch star tip, and pipe the yolk mixture back into the whites. This is a lot easier than using a spoon.) Place the stuffed egg halves on a serving platter, cover loosely with plastic wrap, and refrigerate until serving time, or up to 8 hours.

5. Just before serving, sprinkle the eggs with the chopped pancetta. Serve chilled.

sweet-and-sour vegetables

MAKES ABOUT 1½ QUARTS; 8 TO 10 SERVINGS

When you have a big meal ahead, it is best to keep the antipasti on the light side. That's when it's good to have these marinated vegetables in the refrigerator. They are refreshing, with a sweet-and-sour flavor that keeps you coming back for more. Don't overcook the vegetables, as they will become tender enough from soaking in the hot marinade.

1½ cups water

½ cup chopped yellow onion

½ cup red wine vinegar

¼ cup extra-virgin olive oil

¼ cup sugar

2 tablespoons finely chopped fresh flat-leaf parsley

1 teaspoon dried oregano

2 garlic cloves, finely chopped

1 bay leaf

2 large carrots, cut into ½-inch rounds

2 medium celery ribs, cut into ½-inch slices

1 large zucchini, cut in half lengthwise, and then into ½-inch slices

1 large red bell pepper, cored, seeded, and cut into ½-inch-wide strips

1½ cups thawed frozen baby onions (see Note)

1. Combine the water with the chopped onion, vinegar, oil, sugar, parsley, oregano, garlic, and bay leaf in a large saucepan. Bring the mixture to a boil over high heat, stirring to dissolve the sugar.

2. Add the carrots and celery, return to a boil, then reduce the heat to medium. Cook until the carrots are beginning to soften, about 5 minutes. Stir in the zucchini, bell pepper, and baby onions and bring just to a simmer. Pour the vegetables and the marinade into a bowl and let cool completely.

3. Cover the bowl with plastic wrap and refrigerate until chilled, at least 2 hours and up to 5 days. Remove and discard the bay leaf. Using a slotted spoon, transfer the vegetables to a platter and serve chilled.

Note: Fresh cipollini, small and squat onions available at specialty markets, can be substituted for the thawed frozen onions. To prepare the cipollini, trim off the top and bottom of 12 small cipollini. Bring a medium saucepan of salted water to a boil over high heat. Add the cipollini and cook just until the skins loosen, about 1 minute. Using a slotted spoon, transfer the cipollini to a bowl of cold water and let them cool. Slip off the skins and pierce a slit into the side of each cipollini. Return to the water and reduce the heat to medium-low. Simmer just until the cipollini are barely tender when pierced with the tip of a small, sharp knife, about 10 minutes. Drain, rinse under cold running water, and let cool completely.

clams oreganata

MAKES 24; 4 TO 6 SERVINGS

Clams oreganata, with a spicy oregano crumb topping, is a restaurant dish that is fun to make in your own kitchen. But most recipes start with shucked clams, a chore that is never easy to do at home. However, if you broil the clams just until they open, you can toss the shucking knife away. These are fantastic served with a cold glass of Pinot Grigio.

2 dozen littleneck clams

Kosher salt

½ cup plain dried bread crumbs

1 tablespoon finely chopped fresh flat-leaf parsley

1 teaspoon dried oregano

1 large garlic clove, minced

¼ teaspoon hot red pepper flakes

2 tablespoons extra-virgin olive oil, plus more for drizzling

Lemon wedges, for serving

1. Scrub the clams under cold running water. Soak them in a large bowl of salted ice water for 1 hour. Drain the clams.

2. Position a broiler rack about 8 inches from the heat source and preheat the broiler on high.

3. Arrange the clams on a broiler pan. Broil just until the shells open, 2 to 3 minutes. Discard any clams that do not open. Remove the broiler rack from the oven and let the clams cool until they are easy to handle. Turn off the broiler.

4. Open the clams completely and discard the empty half of the shell. Run a small, sharp knife underneath the clam in each shell to release the meat, leaving the meat in the shell.

5. Mix the bread crumbs, parsley, oregano, garlic, and red pepper flakes together in a small bowl. Stir in the 2 tablespoons of oil to moisten the mixture. Using a dessertspoon, scoop up the crumbs and press them firmly into each clam shell to cover the clam meat. Arrange the clams on the broiler pan, crumbed side up. Drizzle the clams with more oil.

6. Reheat the broiler on high. Return the pan to the broiler and broil until the crumbs are golden brown, watching carefully to avoid burning, 1 to 2 minutes. Using kitchen tongs, transfer the clams to plates and serve immediately, with the lemon wedges.

soups
&
salads

chicken soup
with cheese custard

I never heard Mom say that there was nothing in the house for lunch or dinner. That's because she had learned how to make a lot out of a little. If we had chicken broth, but not chicken meat to go in it, she'd bake these fast Romano cheese custards to float in the vegetable-enhanced soup.

SOUP

1 tablespoon olive oil

1 medium yellow onion, chopped

1 medium carrot, cut into ½-inch dice

6 cups Next-Day Roast Chicken Stock (page 40) or canned reduced-sodium chicken broth

CUSTARDS

8 large eggs

½ cup freshly grated Pecorino Romano cheese (2 ounces)

2 tablespoons olive oil, plus more for the baking dish

2 tablespoons all-purpose flour

1 tablespoon finely chopped fresh flat-leaf parsley

1 teaspoon baking powder

Chopped fresh flat-leaf parsley, for garnish

1. To make the soup: Heat the oil in a large saucepan over medium heat. Add the onion and carrot. Cover and cook, stirring occasionally, until the carrot has softened, about 5 minutes. Add the broth and bring to a boil over high heat. Reduce the heat to medium-low and simmer until the carrot is very tender, about 30 minutes.

2. Meanwhile, make the custards: Position a rack in the center of the oven and preheat the oven to 350°F. Lightly oil an 8 by 11½-inch baking dish.

3. Whisk the eggs, Romano, oil, flour, parsley, and baking powder together in a medium bowl until combined. Pour into the baking dish. Bake until the custard is set and a knife inserted into the center comes out clean, about 15 minutes. Let stand at room temperature for 5 minutes. Cut the custard into bite-size pieces.

4. For each serving, ladle the soup into bowls, add a few warm custards, sprinkle with the chopped parsley, and serve hot.

Stracciatella

You can get a similar flavor to the custards with stracciatella, thin shreds of egg and cheese cooked directly in the soup. Omit the custards. Whisk 2 large eggs with ¼ cup freshly grated Parmesan cheese in a medium bowl. Stirring the simmering soup, add the egg mixture in a stream. Cook until the egg mixture has set into very thin ribbons, about 1 minute.

next-day roast chicken stock

MAKES ABOUT 6 CUPS

My mom, like most of the women in our neighborhood, would never dream of throwing away a perfectly good roast chicken carcass. Instead, she'd toss it in a pot, add a few vegetables, and simmer it with water to make a tasty cooking stock. If you wish, add some canned broth or a bouillon cube for extra flavor. But keep in mind that you are often using the broth in a recipe with ingredients that will provide their own taste, so don't be too concerned if the broth isn't "chicken-y" at first. You can make a good broth with just an onion, so if you don't have the carrot, celery, or parsley, don't let that stop you from "recycling" your chicken.

Carcass from 1 roasted chicken, such as Roast Chicken with Chestnut-Sausage Stuffing (page 129), including the skin, plus neck and any giblets (but not the liver) reserved from the raw chicken

1 tablespoon olive oil

1 small onion, coarsely chopped

1 small carrot, coarsely chopped

1 small celery rib, coarsely chopped

One 13¾-ounce can reduced-sodium chicken broth, or 1 chicken bouillon cube dissolved in 1¾ cups boiling water (optional)

4 sprigs flat-leaf parsley

2 sprigs fresh thyme, or ⅛ teaspoon dried thyme

1 small bay leaf

Kosher salt and freshly ground black pepper

1. If there is any stuffing clinging to the chicken carcass, quickly rinse it off with cold running water. Using your hands, break up the carcass into manageable pieces and set them aside.

2. Heat the oil in a large saucepan over medium heat. Add the onion, carrot, and celery and cook, stirring occasionally, until the onion softens, about 3 minutes. Add the chicken carcass and the neck and giblets, it using. Pour in the canned broth, if using, and enough cold water to barely cover the chicken, about 6 cups. Bring just to a boil over high heat, skimming off any foam that rises to the surface.

3. Add the parsley, thyme, and bay leaf and reduce the heat to low. Simmer, uncovered, until the broth is full-flavored, at least 2 and up to 3 hours. Season to taste with salt and pepper.

4. Strain the broth through a fine mesh-sieve or colander into a large bowl; discard the solids. Let cool to tepid. Cover and refrigerate for up to 3 days, or freeze for up to 3 months.

lentil, sausage, and spinach soup

MAKES 12 SERVINGS

A pound of lentils goes a long way, and this rib-sticking recipe from Mom's notebook makes a huge pot. Go ahead and make the whole batch and freeze it to have on hand for a quick lunch or supper.

4 tablespoons olive oil

1 medium yellow onion, chopped

1 medium red bell pepper, cored, seeded, and chopped

2 garlic cloves, finely chopped

1 pound sweet Italian pork sausage, casings removed

1 pound dried brown lentils, sorted over for stones, rinsed, and drained

3½ cups canned reduced-sodium chicken broth

4 cups water

½ cup dry sherry

1 teaspoon finely chopped fresh thyme, or ½ teaspoon dried thyme

1 teaspoon finely chopped fresh sage, or ½ teaspoon dried sage

Kosher salt

½ teaspoon hot red pepper flakes

1 bay leaf

One 5-ounce bag baby spinach

2 cups hot water

Freshly ground black pepper

1. Heat 2 tablespoons of the oil in a large pot over medium heat. Add the onion, bell pepper, and garlic and cook, stirring occasionally, until softened, about 3 minutes. Transfer the vegetable mixture to a bowl.

2. Add the remaining 2 tablespoons oil to the pot and heat over medium-high heat. Add the sausage and cook, stirring occasionally and breaking up the sausage into bite-size pieces with the side of a wooden spoon, until browned, about 10 minutes. Add the lentils, broth, the 4 cups water, sherry, thyme, sage, 1 teaspoon salt, and the red pepper flakes and bring to a boil over high heat. Reduce the heat to low and simmer until the lentils are barely tender, about 45 minutes.

3. Stir in the spinach and the 2 cups hot water. Return to the simmer over high heat. Reduce the heat to medium-low and simmer until the spinach is very tender, about 5 minutes. Remove and discard the bay leaf. Season to taste with salt and black pepper. Serve hot.

italian wedding soup

MAKES 6 TO 8 SERVINGS

In spite of its name, this is not a soup served at Italian weddings! The name comes from the veal meatballs and vegetables wedded together in a kind of culinary matrimonial bliss. The meatballs should be as small as possible, no more than a teaspoon of the veal mixture for each ball. This wonderful soup always includes "bitter" greens, and as these greens are always sandy, be sure to wash them well before adding them to the simmering broth.

MINI VEAL MEATBALLS

½ cup soft bread crumbs, made from day-old bread

2 tablespoons whole milk

¼ cup freshly grated Pecorino Romano cheese (1 ounce)

1 large egg yolk

1 tablespoon minced fresh flat-leaf parsley

½ teaspoon finely chopped fresh thyme

½ teaspoon kosher salt

¼ teaspoon garlic powder

¼ teaspoon freshly ground black pepper

8 ounces ground veal

2 ounces ground pork, or more ground veal

SOUP

2 tablespoons olive oil

1 medium yellow onion, chopped

1 medium carrot, cut into ½-inch dice

1 medium celery rib, cut into ½-inch dice

6 cups Next-Day Roasted Chicken Stock (page 40) or canned reduced-sodium chicken broth

2 cups water

1 small head escarole, coarsely chopped

1. To make the meatballs: Combine the bread crumbs and milk together in a medium bowl and let stand until the crumbs are softened by the milk, about 3 minutes. Add the Romano, egg yolk, parsley, thyme, salt, garlic powder, and pepper and mix well. Add the veal and pork. Using clean hands, mix the ingredients together just until combined—do not overmix or the meatballs will be heavy. Refrigerate for 15 to 30 minutes so the mixture can firm up a bit.

2. Using wet hands rinsed under cold water, roll a teaspoon of the veal mixture into a small meatball and place on a platter or baking sheet. Repeat with the remaining mixture. Loosely cover the mini meatballs with plastic wrap and refrigerate for at least 30 minutes and up to 2 hours.

3. To make the soup: Heat the oil in a large saucepan over medium heat. Add the onion, carrot, and celery and cover. Cook, stirring occasionally, until the vegetables have softened, about 5 minutes. Stir in the broth and water and bring to a boil over high heat. Reduce the heat to medium-low and simmer, uncovered, until the vegetables are tender, about 15 minutes.

4. Carefully add the meatballs to the simmering soup. Cover and simmer for 5 minutes, just until the meatballs are set. Gently stir in the escarole and return to the simmer. Continue cooking, uncovered, until the escarole is very tender and the meatballs are cooked through, about 15 minutes. Season to taste with salt and freshly ground pepper. Serve hot.

pasta e fagioli

MAKES 8 TO 10 SERVINGS

Pasta e fagioli is one of the classic Italian soups, and can be made with just about any dried beans, although white beans seem to be the most common. The soup is always pronounced in Sicilian dialect as "pasta fazool," and never in the textbook "pasta fahj-ee-oh-lee." Give me a bowl of this on a cold rainy afternoon with a big chunk of bread, and I am instantly warmed up.

1 pound dried cannellini beans, sorted over for stones, rinsed, and drained

Kosher salt

3 tablespoons olive oil

½ cup diced pancetta (2½ ounces)

1 large yellow onion, chopped

1 large carrot, cut into ½-inch dice

1 large celery rib, cut into ½-inch dice

3 garlic cloves, minced

One 13¾-ounce can reduced-sodium chicken broth, or 1¾ cups water

1 smoked pig's foot, split in half by the butcher (see Note)

2 tablespoons finely chopped fresh flat-leaf parsley

1 teaspoon chopped fresh rosemary, or ½ teaspoon dried rosemary

1 teaspoon chopped fresh thyme, or ½ teaspoon dried thyme

2 bay leaves

One 28-ounce can tomatoes in juice, drained with juices reserved, tomatoes coarsely crushed

Kosher salt and freshly ground black pepper

2 cups (8 ounces) ditalini or other short tube-shaped pasta

1. Put the beans in a large bowl and add enough cold water to cover by 2 inches. Let the beans soak at room temperature for at least 4 and up to 8 hours. If the kitchen is hot, refrigerate them. (Or, put the beans in a large saucepan, add enough cold water to cover by 2 inches, and bring to a boil over high heat. Cook for 2 minutes. Remove from the heat, cover, and let stand for 1 hour.) Drain the beans.

2. Heat the oil in a large pot over medium heat. Add the pancetta and cook, stirring occasionally, until the pancetta is lightly browned, about 3 minutes. Stir in the onion, carrot, celery, and garlic and cook, stirring occasionally, until the onion has softened, about 3 minutes. Add the drained beans, broth, and the pig's foot and bring to a boil, skimming off any foam that rises to the surface. Add the parsley, rosemary, thyme, and bay leaves. Add enough water to cover the mixture by 1 inch. Bring to a boil over high heat. Reduce the heat to medium-low and simmer, occasionally skimming off any foam, until the beans are almost tender, skimming as needed, about 45 minutes.

3. Add the tomatoes and their juices and return to the simmer. Continue cooking until the beans are tender, about 30 minutes more.

4. Add hot water to the soup as needed to be sure that the solids are covered by about ½ inch. Season the soup to taste with salt and pepper. Stir in the ditalini and return to a boil over high heat. Reduce the heat to medium-low and cook until the ditalini is very tender, about 15 minutes. Remove and discard the pig's foot and bay leaves. Season the soup again with salt and pepper and serve. (The soup can be cooled, covered, and refrigerated for up to 3 days, or frozen for up to 3 months. When reheating, adjust the consistency with water.)

Note: Smoked pig's feet are sold by many Italian butchers. Because they have a lot of gelatin, they give the soup extra body, as well as flavor. If you wish, substitute 1 pound smoked pork hocks, which are carried by most supermarkets, sawed in half crosswise by the butcher. After removing the pig foot or hocks from the pot, you can let the pieces cool, pick the meat from the bones, and stir the meat back into the soup—but there usually isn't enough meat to bother.

frankie's vegetable minestrone

Here's how I make minestrone. It is loaded with my favorite vegetables, even if they may not be the traditional ones. They produce so much flavor that I usually don't put any meat in the soup, but you can use chicken broth instead of water, if you wish. Just add some crusty bread, and you have one of the best lunches ever.

3 tablespoons olive oil

1 large yellow onion, chopped

1 large carrot, cut into
½-inch dice

1 large celery rib, cut into
½-inch dice

2 garlic cloves, minced

One 6-ounce can tomato paste

3 quarts water

1 large yam, about 9 ounces,
peeled and cut into ¾-inch
pieces

2 teaspoons dried oregano

1 bay leaf

12 ounces broccoli crowns,
cut into florets

6 ounces green beans, cut into
1-inch lengths (about 1½ cups)

1 medium zucchini, cut into
½-inch dice

1 medium yellow squash, cut
into ½-inch dice

Kosher salt and freshly ground
black pepper

1 cup short pasta, such as
ditalini

1. Heat the oil in a large pot over medium heat. Add the onion, carrot, celery, and garlic and cook, stirring occasionally, until the onion has softened, about 3 minutes. Move the vegetables to one side of the pot. Add the tomato paste to the empty side and cook, stirring almost constantly, until it begins to coat the bottom of the pot with a dark brown film, about 2 minutes. Add the water and stir to dissolve the tomato paste. Bring to a boil over high heat.

2. Stir in the yam, oregano, and bay leaf. Then reduce the heat to medium-low and simmer for 30 minutes.

3. Add the broccoli, green beans, zucchini, and yellow squash and cook for 15 minutes. Season to taste with salt and pepper.

4. Add the pasta and cook until the pasta and vegetables are tender, about 15 minutes. Remove and discard the bay leaf. Ladle the soup into bowls and serve hot.

the avalon house salad

MAKES 6 SERVINGS

Every household needs a solid salad dressing that can be prepared in a couple of minutes. This one fits the bill, and is versatile enough that everyone at the table will love it. I suggest serving it on the side so each person can add as much or as little as they like. In my family, there is always someone who is counting calories. We always have a lot of vegetables in the house, and use this combination of greens, tomatoes, and cucumber as the beginning, adding shredded carrots, sliced celery, canned beans or beets, chopped olives, or whatever else that sounds good for tonight's salad.

DRESSING

½ cup extra-virgin olive oil

2 tablespoons balsamic vinegar

2 teaspoons honey

½ teaspoon Dijon mustard

¼ teaspoon kosher salt

⅛ teaspoon freshly ground black pepper

6 ounces mixed baby salad greens (mesclun)

1 cup grape or cherry tomatoes, halved

1 cucumber, peeled and sliced

1. To make the dressing: Shake all of the ingredients together in a covered jar until thickened.

2. Toss the greens, tomatoes, and cucumber together in a large bowl. Serve the salad with the dressing passed on the side.

orange and fennel salad

Crisp, refreshing, and attractive, this salad has it all. You can serve it as a first course, a side dish, or on a buffet. It is especially useful during the winter months when oranges are at their peak, but tomatoes and other vegetables are not at their best, and it is excellent with grilled fish. Because oranges can vary in sweetness, adjust the acidity with a little vinegar, if you wish. I like to use a plastic V-slicer or a mandoline to thinly slice the fennel, but use a knife if you prefer. Just be sure the fennel is very thin.

2 navel oranges

2 tablespoons extra-virgin olive oil

Kosher salt and freshly ground black pepper

2 medium fennel bulbs, about 1¾ pounds

1 small red onion, thinly cut into half-moons

1 tablespoon red wine vinegar (optional)

1. Finely grate the zest from 1 orange into a medium bowl. Using a serrated knife, trim off the top and bottom from the oranges. Working with one at a time, place an orange on end on the work surface, and cut away the skin and thick pith where it meets the flesh, leaving a peeled sphere. Cut the oranges horizontally into ¼-inch rounds. Squeeze enough of the rounds in your hand over a small bowl to obtain 2 tablespoons of juice. Cover and refrigerate the remaining orange rounds.

2. Add the orange juice to the bowl with the zest. Whisk in the oil. Season the dressing to taste with the salt and pepper.

3. Cut off the top stalks from the fennel bulbs. Reserve the fronds and save the stalks for another use. Cut each bulb in half vertically. Using a plastic V-slice, mandoline, or large knife, cut the fennel crosswise into slices about 1/16 inch thick. Transfer to a medium bowl and toss with the dressing. Cover the bowl and marinate for at least 30 minutes and up to 2 hours.

4. Just before serving, taste the salad for acidity, and add the vinegar, if desired. Arrange the orange slices around the perimeter of a serving platter, overlapping if needed. Add the red onion to the fennel and toss. Season the fennel salad to taste with salt and pepper. Spoon the fennel salad over the orange slices so that the slices peek out from under the salad. Coarsely chop a tablespoon or so of the fennel fronds and sprinkle over the salad. Serve chilled.

tomato, cucumber, and basil salad

MAKES 4 TO 6 SERVINGS

This salad looks great and tastes even better, and because it goes so well with many main courses, I make it a lot. It is at its best during the summer when tomatoes are really full of flavor. The secret is a splash of water in the dressing, which I find helps spread the flavors better and tones down the vinegar, too.

2 tablespoons red wine vinegar

2 tablespoons water

½ teaspoon kosher salt, plus more as needed

¼ teaspoon freshly ground black pepper, plus more as needed

¼ cup extra-virgin olive oil

2 large beefsteak tomatoes, each cut into 8 wedges

½ seedless (English) cucumber, cut into ¼-inch rounds

1 small yellow or red onion, cut into thin half-moons

3 tablespoons coarsely chopped fresh basil, plus a basil sprig, for garnish

1. Using a fork, whisk the vinegar and water together in large bowl. Add the salt and pepper and whisk to dissolve the salt. Gradually whisk in the oil.

2. Add the tomatoes, cucumber, and onion and toss well. Season to taste with additional salt and pepper. Let stand for 10 to 30 minutes before serving.

3. Sprinkle in the chopped basil and toss to combine. Garnish with the basil sprig and serve.

dolores hope's antipasti salad

MAKES 8 TO 10 SERVINGS

Bob Hope was a great friend of mine, and my wife Kay was a bridesmaid at his daughter Linda's wedding. Dolores Hope was a legendary hostess, and every buffet featured this enormous salad topped with the goodies that you would find on an antipasto platter—salami, roasted red peppers, olives, cheese, and more. We serve it at our family feasts, and it makes a fantastic lunch, too. Of course, you can add or substitute some of your antipasti favorites (such as roasted beets, cherry tomatoes, or marinated mushrooms), but this is Dolores' original recipe. To make serving go easily, prep and refrigerate all of the components, then arrange the salad just before serving. You will need a really big serving bowl to hold everything.

DRESSING

¼ cup red wine vinegar

½ teaspoon kosher salt

¼ teaspoon freshly ground black pepper

¾ cup olive oil

SALAD

1 large head iceberg lettuce, torn into bite-size pieces

4 celery heart ribs with leaves, thinly sliced

One 15.5-ounce can chickpeas (garbanzo beans), drained and rinsed

Two 12-ounce jars marinated artichoke hearts, drained and coarsely chopped

One 12-ounce jar pepperoncini, drained and cut into thin rings

One 12-ounce jar roasted red bell peppers, cut into strips about ¼ inch wide

8 ounces mozzarella cheese, preferably fresh, cut into bite-size cubes

6 ounces sliced Genoa salami, cut into strips about ½ inch wide

Two 2.25-ounce cans sliced black California olives, drained

½ cup freshly grated Pecorino Romano cheese (2 ounces)

1. To make the dressing: Whisk the vinegar, salt, and black pepper together in a medium bowl. Gradually whisk in the oil.

2. Toss the lettuce and dressing together in a very large serving bowl. Arrange the celery, chickpeas, artichoke hearts, pepperoncini, roasted red peppers, mozzarella, salami, and olives, in an attractive spoke pattern on top of the lettuce. Sprinkle with the grated Pecorino Romano cheese, if desired.

3. Serve immediately, letting the guests serve themselves and choose their favorite toppings.

italian tuna salad with arugula

MAKES 4 SERVINGS

In my opinion, American tuna salad is about the mayonnaise and not about the tuna. You won't find that mistake with the Italian version. Tuna has been an important part of Sicilian life for centuries, and the genuine product from that region has fine flavor and rich texture (see Note). Here, I make it into a big salad for a warm-weather lunch or supper. But sometimes, I'll just put the tuna salad in a crusty roll for the best tuna sandwich ever.

DRESSING

2½ tablespoons fresh lemon juice

½ teaspoon kosher salt

¼ teaspoon freshly ground black pepper

½ cup extra-virgin olive oil

POTATO SALAD

1 pound small red-skinned potatoes, scrubbed

2 tablespoons finely sliced fresh chives

Kosher salt and freshly ground black pepper

TUNA SALAD

Two 5- to 6-ounce cans Italian tuna in olive oil, drained (see Note)

1 small celery stalk, finely chopped

2 tablespoons nonpareil capers, drained and rinsed

2 tablespoons finely chopped fresh flat-leaf parsley

Pinch of hot red pepper flakes

5 ounces baby arugula

2 large ripe tomatoes, cut into ½-inch rounds

2 small cucumbers, scrubbed but unpeeled, cut into ¼-inch rounds

⅔ cup coarsely chopped pitted kalamata olives

1. To make the dressing: Whisk the lemon juice, salt, and pepper in a small bowl to dissolve the salt. Gradually whisk in the oil.

2. To make the potato salad: Put the potatoes in a medium sauce-pan and add enough cold salted water to cover them by 1 inch. Bring to a boil over high heat. Reduce the heat to medium and boil until the potatoes are tender when pierced with the tip of a small, sharp knife, about 20 minutes. Drain and rinse under cold running water. Let cool for a few minutes until easy to handle.

3. Slice the potatoes into thin rounds and transfer them to a medium bowl. Add 3 tablespoons of the dressing to the warm potatoes and toss. Let cool until tepid. (If you are making this for lunch, and want to speed up the cooling, put the bowl in a larger bowl of iced water.) Stir in the chives. Season to taste with the salt and pepper. Cover and refrigerate until ready to serve.

4. To make the tuna salad: Stir the tuna, celery, capers, parsley, and red pepper flakes with 2 tablespoons of the dressing in a medium bowl.

5. Spread out the arugula on a deep serving platter. Heap the tuna in the center of the arugula, and arrange individual mounds of the potato salad, tomatoes, cucumbers, and olives around the tuna. Drizzle the vegetables with the remaining dressing. Present the salad at the table. Toss the salad just before serving.

Note: You will find imported Italian tuna at specialty food stores, Italian delicatessens, and many supermarkets. Look care-fully at the label to be sure that the tuna *is* from Italy, as some supermarket varieties use Southeast Asian fish. Italian canned tuna (packed in cans that average 5.5 ounces) is very good, but Italian tuna packed in jars (about 7 ounces) is even better. If you use the jarred tuna, just add a bit more dressing.

pasta

spaghetti
with veal meatballs

MAKES 4 TO 6 SERVINGS

To me, a truly great meatball has to be made with ground veal, not beef, with just enough pork to add a little extra fat and flavor. Veal contains a lot of gelatin that melts during cooking to give the *polpettine* a juicy texture that you just don't get from hamburger. You might have to order ground veal from your butcher, but it is worth a phone call. My mom would experiment with other meats and cooking methods, and our favorites were the braised and turkey meatball variations below and the calamari version on page 85. This old family recipe makes plenty of meatballs so you can have leftovers for a sandwich or two at another meal.

MEATBALLS

2 cups fresh bread crumbs, made from day-old bread

⅔ cup whole milk

2 tablespoons heavy cream

½ cup freshly grated Pecorino Romano cheese (2 ounces)

3 large eggs, beaten

¼ cup minced fresh flat-leaf parsley

2 teaspoons kosher salt

2 teaspoons finely chopped fresh thyme, or 1 teaspoon dried thyme

1 teaspoon finely chopped fresh sage, or ½ teaspoon dried sage

1 teaspoon garlic powder

1 teaspoon freshly ground black pepper

2 pounds ground veal

6 ounces ground pork

SAUCE

3 tablespoons olive oil

1 medium yellow onion, chopped

2 garlic cloves, minced

(INGREDIENTS CONTINUE)

1. To make the meatballs: Combine the bread crumbs, milk, and cream together in a medium bowl and let stand until the crumbs are softened by the milk, about 3 minutes. Add the Romano, eggs, parsley, salt, thyme, sage, garlic powder, and black pepper, and mix well. Add the veal and pork. Using your hands, mix the ingredients together just until combined—do not overmix or the meatballs will be heavy. Refrigerate for 15 to 30 minutes so the mixture can firm up a bit.

2. Using wet hands rinsed under cold water, and scooping about 2 tablespoons of the meat mixture for each meatball, divide and shape the meat mixture into 24 equal meatballs (you can use a food portion scoop, if you wish) and place them on a platter or baking sheet. Loosely cover the meatballs with plastic wrap and refrigerate for 30 minutes to 2 hours.

3. Meanwhile, start the sauce: Heat the oil in a large heavy-bottomed saucepan over medium heat. Add the onion and cook, stirring occasionally, until softened, about 3 minutes. Stir in the garlic and cook until it is fragrant, about 1 minute. Add the wine and bring to a boil. Stir in the tomatoes, water, oregano, red pepper flakes, and bay leaf. Bring to a simmer over medium-high heat, stirring often. Reduce the heat to medium-low and simmer, stirring occasionally, for about 20 minutes.

4. Heat the oil in a large heavy skillet over medium heat. Working in batches without crowding, add the meatballs and cook, turning occasionally and adding more oil to the skillet as needed, until they are browned, 6 to 8 minutes. (Wait for a

(RECIPE CONTINUES)

1 cup hearty red wine, such as Chianti or Shiraz

One 28-ounce can crushed tomatoes

1 cup water

2 teaspoons dried oregano

½ teaspoon hot red pepper flakes

1 bay leaf

Kosher salt

⅔ cup coarsely chopped fresh basil

1 pound spaghetti

Freshly grated Pecorino Romano cheese, for serving

crust to form on the underside of the meatballs before turning them.) Using a slotted spoon, transfer the meatballs to a plate. Pour off the fat in the skillet. Add about ½ cup water to the skillet and bring to a boil, scraping up the browned bits from the bottom with a wooden spoon. Stir the deglazed mixture into the sauce.

5. Carefully add the meatballs to the sauce, making sure they are submerged in the sauce. (Add more hot water to the sauce, if needed.) Adjust the heat so the sauce is simmering and partially cover the saucepan to keep the sauce from reducing too quickly. Cook, occasionally stirring to avoid scorching, until the meatballs are cooked through and the sauce has thickened slightly, about 45 minutes. During the last 10 minutes, stir in the basil.

6. Meanwhile, bring a large pot of salted water to a boil over high heat. Add the spaghetti and cook, according to the package directions, until al dente. Drain well and return the spaghetti to the cooking pot.

7. Using a slotted spoon, transfer the meatballs to a serving platter. Remove and discard the bay leaf from the sauce. Stir about 3 cups of the sauce into the spaghetti. Transfer the spaghetti to a serving bowl and top with the remaining sauce. Serve immediately with the meatballs, and the Romano passed on the side.

Turkey Meatballs

Substitute regular ground turkey (93 percent lean, not extra-lean ground turkey breast) for the veal.

Braised Meatballs

Many fine cooks swear by this method, which skips the browning step and ensures tender, melt-in-your-mouth meatballs. After the sauce has simmered for about 20 minutes, one at a time, drop the raw meatballs into the simmering sauce, letting each meatball cook for about 15 seconds to firm slightly before adding another. Be careful when moving the meatballs while making room for more in the saucepan to avoid breaking them. Once the meatballs have been added, adjust the heat so the sauce is simmering, and cook as directed.

sicilian chicken meatballs in rosemary-tomato sauce

MAKES 4 TO 6 SERVINGS

When I first started performing in Las Vegas, Villa d' Este was *the* Italian restaurant. It was just as much a social club as it was a place to eat, and I would run into every Italian entertainer, from Dean Martin to Connie Francis, who happened to be in town. I always ordered these chicken meatballs with their Sicilian flavors of currants, pine nuts, and parsley in every bite. These meatballs are delicate, so don't manhandle them when cooking.

MEATBALLS

3 tablespoons pine nuts

3 tablespoons dried currants

1½ cups soft bread crumbs, made from slightly stale bread

¼ cup whole milk

⅔ cup minced yellow onion

1 large egg, beaten

2 tablespoons finely chopped fresh flat-leaf parsley

1 garlic clove, minced

1 teaspoon kosher salt

½ teaspoon freshly ground black pepper

1 pound ground chicken (not extra-lean)

2 tablespoons olive oil, plus more as needed

SAUCE

2 tablespoons olive oil

1 medium yellow onion, finely chopped

2 garlic cloves, minced

2 tablespoons tomato paste

½ cup dry white wine

One 28-ounce can crushed tomatoes

¾ cup water

1. To make the meatballs: Toast the pine nuts in a small skillet over medium heat, stirring occasionally, until toasted, about 3 minutes. Transfer the pine nuts to a plate and let them cool.

2. Soak the currants in hot tap water to cover in a small bowl until they are plumped and softened, about 10 minutes. Drain them well and pat dry with paper towels.

3. Mix the bread crumbs and milk together in a medium bowl and let stand until the crumbs have softened. Add the onion, egg, pine nuts, drained currants, parsley, garlic, salt, and pepper and stir well to incorporate the egg. Add the chicken and mix with your clean hands just until combined—do not overhandle the mixture. Refrigerate for 15 to 30 minutes so the mixture can firm up a bit.

4. Using wet hands, divide and shape the chicken mixture into 12 meatballs, and place them on a large baking sheet. Heat the oil in a large nonstick skillet over medium heat. Working in batches, without crowding, add the meatballs and cook, turning them occasionally and adding more oil as needed, until lightly browned, about 6 minutes. Return the meatballs to the baking sheet.

5. To make the sauce: Heat the oil in a large heavy bottomed saucepan over medium heat. Add the onion and cook, stirring occasionally, until has softened, about 3 minutes. Stir in the garlic and cook until it is fragrant, about 1 minute. Move the vegetables to one side of the pot. Add the tomato paste to the empty side of the pot and stir until it toasts and coats the bottom of the pot with a dark, thin film, about 1 minute.

1 tablespoon finely chopped
fresh rosemary, or 1½
teaspoons dried rosemary

Kosher salt and freshly ground
black pepper

1 pound spaghetti

Freshly grated Pecorino
Romano, for serving

6. Pour in the wine and stir to combine with the vegetables and dissolve the paste. Stir in the tomatoes, water, and rosemary. Bring to a boil, stirring often. Add the meatballs and any juices on the baking sheet to the sauce. Reduce the heat to medium-low. Simmer, uncovered, stirring occasionally and gently to avoid breaking the meatballs, until they show no sign of pink when pierced to the center with the tip of a small sharp knife, and the sauce has reduced slightly, about 45 minutes. Season the sauce to taste with salt and pepper.

7. Meanwhile, bring a large pot of salted water to a boil over high heat. Add the spaghetti and cook, according to the package directions, until al dente. Drain well.

8. Return the pasta to its cooking pot. Stir in a cup or two of the sauce. Transfer the pasta to a large serving bowl and top with the remaining sauce and the meatballs. Serve with the Romano passed on the side.

sunday gravy
with meatballs, sausage, and ribs

MAKES 8 TO 12 SERVINGS

Virtually every Italian-American family has the tradition of Sunday "gravy," a sauce that simmers all day with a collection of meats to give it an incredible flavor. There are many variations—some people include braciole or a cut of pot roast, and some use pork neck instead of spareribs. But, for my version, I have settled on spareribs, sausage, and meatballs. You will need a very big Dutch oven (one with at least a 7-quart capacity) to hold everything, and a huge pot to cook two pounds of pasta. In the kitchens of most of the Italian families I know, these are standard equipment.

8 tablespoons olive oil

3 pounds spareribs, cut by the butcher vertically in half, and then into individual ribs

1 teaspoon kosher salt, plus more as needed

¾ teaspoon freshly ground black pepper, plus more as needed

2 medium yellow onions, chopped

1 large carrot, cut into ½-inch dice

2 medium celery ribs, cut into ½-inch dice

6 garlic cloves, minced

1½ cups hearty red wine, such as Shiraz

Two 28-ounce cans crushed tomatoes

3 cups water

1 tablespoon plus 1 teaspoon dried oregano

½ teaspoon hot red pepper flakes

2 bay leaves

1½ pounds sweet Italian pork sausage, pierced with a fork

½ recipe Veal Meatballs (page 62)

1. Heat 2 tablespoons of the oil in a very large Dutch oven over medium-high heat. Season the spareribs with the 1 teaspoon salt and ¾ teaspoon black pepper. Working in batches without crowding, add the spareribs to the oil and cook, turning occasionally, until browned, about 6 minutes. Transfer to a platter.

2. Add 2 tablespoons of the remaining oil to the Dutch oven and heat it. Add the onion, carrot, and celery and reduce the heat to medium. Cover and cook, stirring occasionally, until the vegetables have softened, about 6 minutes. Stir in the garlic and cook, uncovered, until the onion is golden, about 2 minutes more. Stir in the wine and bring to a boil.

3. Add the crushed tomatoes, water, oregano, red pepper flakes, and bay leaves and bring to a boil over high heat. Reduce the heat to medium-low and simmer for 30 minutes.

4. Heat 2 tablespoons of the remaining oil in a large skillet over medium-high heat. Add the sausage and cook, turning occasionally, until browned, about 6 minutes. Add to the tomato sauce. Add about ½ cup water to the skillet and bring to a boil, scraping up any browned bits from the bottom with a wooden spoon. Stir into the tomato sauce. Simmer the sauce for 1 hour. Wash and dry the skillet.

5. Heat the remaining 2 tablespoons oil in the skillet over medium-high heat. Working in batches without crowding, add the meatballs and cook, turning occasionally (wait for them to form a crust on the underside before turning), until browned on all sides, about 8 minutes. Transfer the meatballs to a platter.

2 pounds ziti, or other tube-shaped pasta

Freshly grated Pecorino Romano cheese, for serving

6. Gently stir the meatballs into the sauce, making sure that they are submerged and adding hot water as needed. Simmer until the meatballs are cooked through, 30 to 40 minutes.

7. Meanwhile, bring a stockpot of salted water to a boil over high heat. Reduce the heat to low to keep it at a simmer until ready to cook the pasta.

8. Using a slotted spoon, transfer the spareribs, sausage, and meatballs to a very large platter. Cut each sausage in half crosswise. Add about ½ cup of the sauce to the platter and cover it with aluminum foil to keep it warm. Increase the heat to medium-high and cook the sauce, stirring often, until it has thickened and reduced by about one-quarter, about 15 minutes. Season to taste with additional salt and pepper as needed.

9. Increase the heat under the stockpot to high to return the salted water to a boil. Add the ziti and cook, according to the package directions, until al dente. Drain well and return the ziti to the cooking pot. Add about 4 cups of the sauce to the ziti, mix well, and transfer to a large serving bowl. Pour the remaining sauce into a serving bowl.

10. Serve the ziti with the meats and the Pecorino Romano passed on the side.

ziti
with broccoli rabe and sausage

MAKES 4 TO 6 SERVINGS

Broccoli rabe can be a take-it-or-leave-it vegetable, but most Italians love its spicy taste. It can be blanched to remove some of its bite, and this is a good way to serve it to kids and others who might prefer a milder flavor. If you like your broccoli rabe in all its hot and spicy glory, just add it (still wet from rinsing) to the skillet and cook it, covered, until al dente, 6 to 8 minutes. Broccoli rabe is fantastic with sausage, and maybe at its very best as a pasta sauce.

Kosher salt

1¼ pounds broccoli rabe, cut into 1- to 2-inch pieces

2 tablespoons olive oil

1 pound sweet Italian pork sausage, casings removed

2 garlic cloves, finely chopped

½ teaspoon hot red pepper flakes

1 pound ziti, or other tube-shaped pasta

½ cup freshly grated Pecorino Romano cheese (2 ounces), plus more for serving

1. Bring a large saucepan of salted water to a boil over high heat. Add the broccoli rabe and cook until crisp-tender, about 5 minutes. Drain well.

2. Bring a large pot of salted water to a boil over high heat.

3. Meanwhile, heat the oil in a large skillet over medium heat. Add the sausage and cook, stirring occasionally and breaking up the sausage into bite-size pieces with the side of a wooden spoon, until the sausage is beginning to brown, about 10 minutes. Stir in the garlic and red pepper flakes and cook until the garlic is fragrant, about 1 minute. Add the broccoli rabe and cook, stirring occasionally, until the broccoli rabe is tender, about 5 minutes. Remove from the heat and cover to keep warm.

4. Add the ziti to the pot of boiling water and cook, according to the package directions, until al dente. Scoop out and reserve about ½ cup of the pasta cooking water. Drain the ziti in a colander and return the ziti to its cooking pot. Add the sausage mixture and the Romano. Mix well, stirring in enough of the pasta cooking water to make a light sauce. Season to taste with salt. Serve hot, with the additional Romano passed on the side.

sausage and cheese lasagna

MAKES 9 SERVINGS

I know a lot of people who are extremely proud of their family's lasagna, and I think I can say that I never met a lasagna I didn't like. But this is lasagna to *love*. It touches all of the bases to score a home run. There is a simple explanation for this—I use sausage in the sauce, and not the common beef. Oh, and fresh mozzarella and ricotta are two other not-so-secret ingredients.

FILLING

2 pounds fresh ricotta cheese, drained (see page 6)

1 cup freshly grated Pecorino Romano cheese (4 ounces)

2 large eggs, beaten

2 tablespoons finely chopped fresh flat-leaf parsley

1 teaspoon kosher salt

½ teaspoon freshly ground black pepper

16 dried lasagna noodles (about 12 ounces)

Olive oil, for the pasta and baking dish

1 recipe Sausage Marinara (page 90), sausage well crumbled

1 pound fresh mozzarella cheese, cut into small cubes

¼ cup freshly grated Pecorino Romano cheese (1 ounce)

1. To make the filling: Mix the ricotta, Romano, eggs, parsley, salt, and pepper together in a large bowl. Cover and refrigerate until ready to use.

2. Bring a large pot of salted water to a boil over high heat. Add the lasagna noodles and cook, according to the package directions, until barely al dente. Do not overcook the noodles because they will be baked in the oven and you don't want them to be mushy. Drain and rinse under cold running water. Drizzle lightly with the oil and toss in the colander to keep the lasagna from sticking together. (This is the only time you are ever going to hear me recommend adding oil to pasta!)

3. Position a rack in the center of the oven and preheat the oven to 350°F. Oil a 9 by 13-inch baking dish.

4. Spread ½ cup of the sauce in the bottom of the prepared baking dish. Arrange 4 noodles in the dish, and top with one-third of the ricotta filling, one-quarter of the mozzarella, and 1 cup of the sauce, distributing them as evenly as possible over the noodles. Repeat twice. Finish with the remaining noodles, spread with the remaining sauce, and sprinkle with the remaining mozzarella. Top with the Romano. (The lasagna can be covered with oiled aluminum foil, oiled side down, and refrigerated for up to 8 hours before baking.)

5. Place the baking dish on a large rimmed baking sheet. Bake for 30 minutes. Uncover and continue baking until the lasagna is bubbling throughout, 30 to 45 minutes longer. Let stand for 10 minutes. Cut into 9 pieces and serve.

rigatoni
with sausage, peppers, and ricotta

MAKES 4 TO 6 SERVINGS

I think of this as pasta for grown-ups. It takes the old favorite, sausage and peppers, to another level by turning it into a pasta sauce, finished off by a dollop of ricotta. (Take the cheese out of the refrigerator a hour or so before serving to remove its chill before it goes onto the ziti.) This is a good dish for eating in front of the TV watching the game (we're Dodgers fans at my house), with a big glass of red wine alongside.

SAUCE

2 tablespoons olive oil, plus more as needed

12 ounces hot Italian sausage, casings removed

1 medium yellow onion, chopped

1 medium red bell pepper, cored, seeded, and cut into ½-inch dice

2 garlic cloves

One 28-ounce can tomatoes in juice, coarsely crushed, juices reserved

½ cup hearty red wine, such as Chianti or Shiraz

3 tablespoons tomato paste

2 teaspoons dried oregano

½ teaspoon hot red pepper flakes

1 bay leaf

¼ cup coarsely chopped pitted kalamata olives

3 tablespoons nonpareil capers, drained and rinsed

Kosher salt

1 pound rigatoni

1½ cups ricotta cheese, at room temperature

1. To make the sauce: Heat the oil in a large heavy-bottomed saucepan over medium heat. Add the sausage and cook, stirring occasionally and breaking up the sausage into bite-size pieces with the side of a wooden spoon, until the sausage has browned, about 8 minutes. Using a slotted spoon, transfer the sausage to a bowl, leaving the fat in the saucepan.

2. Add more oil to the saucepan, if needed. Add the onion and bell pepper and reduce the heat to medium. Cook, stirring occasionally, until the vegetables are tender, about 5 minutes. Stir in the garlic and cook until fragrant, about 1 minute. Stir in the tomatoes with their juices, the wine, tomato paste, oregano, red pepper flakes, and bay leaf. Return the sausage to the saucepan. Bring to a boil. Reduce the heat to medium-low. Simmer, stirring often, until the sauce has reduced by about one-quarter, about 45 minutes. During the last 5 minutes, stir in the olives and capers. Remove and discard the bay leaf. Season to taste with the salt.

3. Bring a large pot of salted water to a boil over high heat. Add the rigatoni and cook, according to the package directions, until al dente. Drain. Return the rigatoni to its cooking pot. Add the sauce and stir well.

4. Spoon the pasta into bowls. Top each with serving with a large dollop of ricotta, and serve with the freshly grated Pecorino Romano or Parmesan cheese, passed on the side.

pasta e ceci

MAKES 4 SERVINGS

Say "pastachechee" to anyone in my family, and their eyes light up. It isn't the most familiar pasta dish, but it is the ultimate comfort food to many Italians, eaten by the spoonful out of a big bowl. *Ceci* means "chickpeas" in Italian, and they are the main event here. Note that the pasta is cooked right in the sauce with the beans to make a kind of thick soup.

2 tablespoons olive oil

1 medium yellow onion, chopped

2 garlic cloves, finely chopped

One 28-ounce can plum tomatoes in juice, coarsely chopped, juices reserved

2 teaspoons finely chopped fresh rosemary, or 1 teaspoon dried rosemary

1 teaspoon kosher salt, plus more as needed

¼ teaspoon hot red pepper flakes

1 bay leaf

Two 15-ounce cans chickpeas (garbanzo beans)

1 cup canned reduced-sodium chicken broth

2 cups ditalini, or other short tube-shaped pasta

Chopped fresh rosemary or flat-leaf parsley, for serving

Freshly grated Parmesan cheese, for serving

1. Heat the oil in a large heavy-bottomed saucepan over medium heat. Add the onion and cook, stirring occasionally, until the onion is golden, about 4 minutes. Stir in the garlic and cook until fragrant, about 1 minute. Stir in the tomatoes with their juices, and the rosemary, the 1 teaspoon salt, red pepper flakes, and the bay leaf. Bring to a boil. Reduce the heat to medium and cook at a brisk simmer, stirring occasionally, until the tomato juices have thickened, about 15 minutes.

2. Drain the chickpeas, reserving the liquid. In a blender, purée half of the chickpeas with all of their reserved liquid. Set the remaining chickpeas aside. Stir the bean purée and chicken broth into the tomato sauce and bring to a simmer over high heat. Season to taste with additional salt if needed.

3. Stir in the ditalini and reserved chickpeas and return to a simmer. Reduce the heat to medium and cook at a steady simmer, stirring almost constantly, until the mixture is thick and the pasta is tender, about 12 minutes. Season to taste with salt if needed. Remove and discard the bay leaf.

4. Spoon into bowls and sprinkle with the rosemary. Serve hot with the Parmesan passed on the side.

stuffed shells
with three cheeses and basil

MAKES 4 TO 6 SERVINGS

Whenever I see stuffed shells on a menu, I am tempted to order them, and I often succumb to temptation. This recipe uses ricotta, mozzarella, and Romano in the filling, with the addition of fragrant basil to put it over the top. I am careful not to fill the shells too much, or they get too rich.

STUFFING

1 pound fresh ricotta cheese, drained

2 cups finely chopped fresh mozzarella cheese (10 ounces)

½ cup freshly grated Pecorino Romano cheese (2 ounces)

¼ cup finely chopped fresh basil, or 2 tablespoons finely chopped fresh flat-leaf parsley

¼ teaspoon freshly ground black pepper

⅛ teaspoon freshly grated nutmeg

Kosher salt

1 large egg, beaten

1 pound jumbo pasta shells for stuffing

Olive oil, for the baking dish

1 recipe Red Wine Marinara Sauce (page 90)

1 cup finely chopped fresh mozzarella cheese (5 ounces)

3 tablespoons freshly grated Pecorino Romano cheese

1. To make the stuffing: Mix the ricotta, mozzarella, Romano, basil, pepper, and nutmeg together in a large bowl. Season to taste with salt. Stir in the egg.

2. Meanwhile, bring a large pot of salted water to a boil over high heat. Add the shells and cook, according to the package directions, until al dente. Drain, rinse under cold running water, and drain again.

3. Lightly oil a 9 by 13-inch baking dish. Spread the marinara sauce in the dish. Using a dessertspoon, divide the stuffing among the pasta shells, filling them equally. (Or transfer the stuffing to a pastry bag fitted with a ½-inch plain pastry tip, and pipe the filling into the shells.) Arrange the shells in the sauce in the baking dish. Top with the mozzarella and Romano. Cover the dish with aluminum foil. (The shells can be refrigerated for up to 6 hours before baking.)

4. Bake for 30 minutes. Uncover and bake until the sauce is bubbling throughout and the cheese has melted, about 15 minutes more. Let stand for 5 minutes. Serve hot.

classic fettuccine alfredo

MAKES 4 TO 6 SERVINGS

Growing up, pasta meant red sauce of some kind, or maybe a meaty Bolognese sauce. So, when Kay and I were on our honeymoon in Mexico City, we came across the unfamiliar fettuccine Alfredo on a menu. (One might expect to find it in Italy, but not Mexico! But remember that this was when the "continental restaurant" was in its heyday.) We gave it a try, and it was love at first bite. Back then, the dish was prepared tableside in a chafing dish to ensure that the pasta was served piping hot. These days, I make it on the stovetop in a big skillet. Mix the ingredients in the specified order so the cheese melts smoothly—just don't dump everything in and expect perfection.

1 pound dried fettuccine

8 tablespoons (1 stick) unsalted butter

2 cups heavy cream

1 large egg yolk

2 cups freshly grated Parmesan cheese (8 ounces), plus more for serving

Freshly ground black pepper

1. Bring a large pot of salted water to a boil over high heat. Add the fettuccine and cook, according to the package directions, until al dente. Drain well.

2. Meanwhile, melt the butter in a large deep skillet over medium-low heat. Add the cream and bring to a simmer. Reduce the heat to very low to keep the cream mixture hot.

3. Beat the egg yolk in a small bowl. Gradually beat in a few tablespoons of the hot cream mixture, and set the yolk mixture aside.

4. Drain the fettuccine well. Add it to the skillet with the cream mixture and toss with tongs to coat. Sprinkle in half of the Parmesan and toss again to melt the cheese. Add the yolk mixture and the remaining Parmesan, and toss again—the heat will cook the yolk; do not let the sauce boil. Season to taste with pepper.

5. Divide the fettuccine among serving bowls and serve immediately with the Parmesan passed on the side.

fettuccine
with shrimp and creamy lemon sauce

MAKES 4 TO 6 SERVINGS

We don't serve creamy pasta very often in our family, only for very special occasions and not weeknight meals. But when you want to indulge a little, try this great dish with shrimp in a sinful cream sauce. The lemon helps to cut through the richness. Serve it in small portions as an appetizer at a dinner party, or dig into a larger serving when you are especially hungry.

2 tablespoons unsalted butter

1½ pounds large shrimp (31–35 count), peeled and deveined

1/3 cup chopped shallots

Grated zest of 1 large lemon

3 tablespoons fresh lemon juice (about 1½ lemons)

2 cups heavy cream

¾ cup canned reduced-sodium chicken broth

4 teaspoons finely chopped fresh rosemary

1 pound dried fettuccine

Kosher salt and freshly ground black pepper

Rosemary sprigs, for garnish

1. Melt 1 tablespoon of the butter in a large skillet over medium-high heat. Add the shrimp. Cook, stirring occasionally, just until they turn opaque, about 2 minutes. Do not overcook the shrimp at this point as they will cook more later. Transfer the shrimp to a plate.

2. Melt the remaining 1 tablespoon butter in the skillet. Add the shallots and cook, stirring often, until softened. Add the lemon zest and juice—the juice will immediately evaporate into a glaze. Stir in the heavy cream, broth, and chopped rosemary. Bring to a boil and cook until the sauce has reduced to about 1¾ cups, 5 to 7 minutes. During the last minute, return the shrimp to the skillet. Season the sauce to taste with salt and pepper.

3. Meanwhile, bring a large pot of salted water to a boil over high heat. Add the fettuccine and cook just until tender, about 9 minutes. Drain well. Return the fettuccine to the pot. Add the sauce and mix well.

4. Serve hot in individual bowls, garnished with the rosemary sprigs.

linguine
with clams and pancetta

MAKES 4 SERVINGS

There is nothing like digging into a steaming bowl of spicy and garlicky linguine with juicy clams. Mom's was better than anyone else's, and having found the recipe in her notebook, I can see why—it's the pancetta. Timing is everything with this sauce, as you want the pasta and sauce to be done at the same time. Be sure to scrub the clams well, and then soak them for an hour or so before cooking. These two steps ensure that dinner won't be ruined by sand hiding in the sauce.

36 littleneck clams, scrubbed well under cold running water

2 tablespoons olive oil

⅔ cup finely diced pancetta

3 garlic cloves, finely chopped

½ teaspoon hot red pepper flakes

1 cup dry white wine, such as Pinot Grigio

2 tablespoons finely chopped fresh flat-leaf parsley, plus more for serving

2 tablespoons cold unsalted butter, cut into ½-inch cubes

1 pound linguine or spaghetti

1. Put the clams in a large bowl and add enough salted ice water to cover. Let stand for 1 hour. Drain the clams.

2. Bring a large pot of salted water to a boil over high heat.

3. Heat the oil in a large saucepan over medium heat. Add the pancetta and cook, stirring occasionally, until lightly browned, about 3 minutes. Add the garlic and stir until the garlic is just beginning to turn golden brown, about 1 minute. Stir in the red pepper flakes, followed by the wine and the 2 tablespoons parsley.

4. Add the spaghetti to the pot of boiling water and cook, according the package directions, until al dente.

5. Meanwhile, add the clams to the saucepan with the wine and increase the heat to high. Cover tightly and cook, occasionally shaking the saucepan, until the clams open, about 8 to 10 minutes. Remove from the heat and discard any unopened clams.

6. Using tongs, transfer the clams to a large bowl. Off the heat, add the butter to the cooking juices and whisk it in. Drain the spaghetti and return it to its cooking pot. Add the sauce and mix well. Divide the pasta and its sauce among four bowls and top each with 9 clams. Sprinkle with the remaining parsley and serve immediately.

spaghetti
with crab marinara

MAKES 4 TO 6 SERVINGS

Crab marinara is one of my family's favorite dishes, and the kids (especially my sons) fight over who's going to get the crab shells to harvest the meat inside. You can serve the legs with the pasta, passed separately, although they are also good—and easier to eat—when cold. If you live on the West Coast, you'll find fresh crab in season in the winter and early spring (or frozen year-round). On the East Coast, see the Note below on how to substitute blue crab.

SAUCE

One 1½ to 2-pounds freshly cooked or thawed frozen Dungeness crab, cleaned and cracked by the fish store (see Note)

3 tablespoons olive oil

One 28-ounce can tomato purée or crushed tomatoes

One 8-ounce bottle clam juice

One 6-ounce can crabmeat (see Note), undrained

1 teaspoon garlic powder

Kosher salt and freshly ground black pepper

1 pound spaghetti

1. Heat the oil in a large heavy-bottomed saucepan over high heat until the oil is very hot. Add the cracked crab in the shell and turn to coat with the oil. Add the tomato purée, clam juice, canned crabmeat with its juices, and garlic powder.

2. Bring to a simmer over medium-high heat. Reduce the heat to medium-low and cook, stirring occasionally, until the sauce has reduced slightly, about 1 hour. Season to taste with salt and pepper.

3. Meanwhile, bring a large pot of salted water to a boil over high heat. Add the spaghetti and cook, according to the package directions, until al dente. Drain the spaghetti and return it to its cooking pot.

4. Using tongs, transfer the crab in the shell to a platter. Add the sauce to the spaghetti and mix well. Divide the spaghetti among serving bowls and serve hot, with the crab passed on the side. (Or cool, cover, and refrigerate the crab and eat it chilled at another meal.)

Notes: Twelve blue crabs, cleaned by the fish store, can be substituted for the Dungeness crabs. To cook, heat 3 tablespoons of olive oil in a large skillet over high heat until the oil is very hot. Working in batches, and adding more oil as needed, add the crabs and cover the skillet (the crabs will "spit" as they cook). Cook, turning occasionally, until the shells turn red, about 5 minutes. It is more difficult to get the meat out of the smaller blue crab shells, so you might not want to bother, but they will season the sauce well.

If you wish, substitute one 8-ounce can refrigerated pasteurized lump crabmeat, picked over for shells and cartilage, for the standard canned crabmeat.

calamari "meatballs"
with spaghetti

MAKES 4 TO 6 SERVINGS

Since my father was a butcher, we had plenty of meat in the house. But, being Catholic, there were also many times when eating meat was forbidden. On these occasions, Mom would run calamari through the meat grinder to make "meatballs" to serve with spaghetti and marinara. Please give these a try—you just might like them as much as the meat kind.

"MEATBALLS"

1 pound cleaned calamari, with or without tentacles, coarsely chopped in 1- to 2-inch pieces

1¼ cups dried Italian-seasoned bread crumbs

1 large egg, beaten

2 tablespoons finely chopped fresh flat-leaf parsley

1 teaspoon dried oregano

1 teaspoon kosher salt

½ teaspoon garlic powder

½ teaspoon freshly ground black pepper

3 tablespoons olive oil

1 recipe White Wine Marinara Sauce (page 90) or Fra Diavolo Sauce (page 150)

1 pound spaghetti

1. To make the meatballs: Pulse the calamari in a food processor until it is almost a paste—don't worry if some small pieces of calamari are visible. Add the bread crumbs, egg, parsley, oregano, salt, garlic powder, and pepper and pulse until the mixture is combined. Scrape it into a bowl, cover with plastic wrap, and refrigerate for 15 to 30 minutes.

2. Using wet hands rinsed under cold water, shape the mixture into 12 equal balls and place them on a platter or baking sheet. Loosely cover the balls with plastic wrap and refrigerate for at least 15 minutes and up to 2 hours.

3. Heat the oil in a large heavy skillet over medium heat. Working in batches without crowding, add the "meatballs" to the skillet and cook, turning occasionally, adding more oil as needed, until they are browned, 6 to 8 minutes. (Wait for a crust to form on the undersides before turning them.) Using a slotted spoon, transfer the "meatballs" to a plate.

4. Bring the sauce to a simmer in a large heavy-bottomed saucepan. Carefully add the "meatballs" to the sauce, making sure they are submerged in the sauce. (Add hot water to the sauce, if needed.) Adjust the heat so the sauce is simmering, and partially cover the saucepan. Cook, stirring occasionally to avoid scorching, until the "meatballs" have cooked through and the sauce has thickened slightly, about 30 minutes.

5. Meanwhile, bring a large pot of salted water to a boil over high heat. Add the spaghetti and cook, according to the package directions, until al dente. Drain well and return the spaghetti to the cooking pot.

6. Using a slotted spoon, transfer the "meatballs" to a serving platter. Stir the sauce into the spaghetti. Transfer the spaghetti to a serving bowl, top with balls, and serve immediately.

potato gnocchi
with pesto

MAKES 6 SERVINGS

Fresh pasta is a labor of love, and most people only make it for special occasions. But gnocchi, which is really a kind of pasta, are much easier to make. Here they are paired with pesto, that mouthwatering sauce that makes everything it touches taste even better. You can also serve gnocchi with just melted butter and a generous sprinkle of Parmesan. Gnocchi are too delicate for tomato sauce.

....

PESTO

1 garlic clove, crushed under a knife and peeled

¼ cup pine nuts

2 cups packed fresh basil leaves

¼ cup freshly grated Parmesan cheese (1 ounce)

¼ cup freshly grated Pecorino Romano cheese or additional Parmesan (1 ounce)

½ cup extra-virgin olive oil, plus more for storing (and if making in a blender)

Kosher salt and freshly ground black pepper.

GNOCCHI

2 pounds baking potatoes, such as russet, peeled

1½ cups unbleached all-purpose flour, plus more as needed and for shaping the gnocchi

1 teaspoon kosher salt

2 large eggs, beaten

½ cup Pesto (see above)

Freshly grated Parmesan cheese, for serving

1. To make the pesto: With the machine running, drop the garlic through the feed tube of a food processor to mince it. Add the pine nuts and pulse until the nuts are finely chopped. Add the basil and the Parmesan and Romano cheeses. Pulse until the basil is minced. With the machine running, gradually pour the oil through the feed tube to make a coarse paste. (Or, combine all of the ingredients in a blender and process, stopping the machine occasionally to scrape down the sides of the jar, and process into a paste, adding more oil if necessary.) Season to taste with salt and pepper. The pesto can be used immediately or refrigerated in a covered container, with a thin layer of olive oil poured on top to "seal" the pesto, for up to 1 month. Stir well before using. (Makes about 1¼ cups.)

2. To make the gnocchi: Put the potatoes in a large saucepan and add enough cold salted water to cover by 1 inch. Cover and bring to a boil over high heat. Reduce the heat to medium, set the lid ajar, and cook at a steady simmer until the potatoes are tender when pierced with the tip of a small sharp knife, about 25 minutes. Drain the potatoes and return them to the saucepan. Cook over low heat, stirring often and breaking the potatoes up with the spoon, until they begin to film the bottom of the saucepan, about 2 minutes. (This forces excess steam out of the potatoes and dries them out a little.)

3. Transfer the potatoes to a large bowl. Force the potatoes through a coarse-mesh wire sieve into a large bowl. Add the flour and salt and stir. Gradually stir in the eggs to make a soft dough that holds its shape when pressed together. Adjust the

(RECIPE CONTINUES)

consistency with more flour, if necessary. Shape the dough into a ball and place it on a floured work surface. Loosely cover the dough with plastic wrap.

4. Flour two large rimmed baking sheets. Cut the dough into sixths. Working with one portion at a time, and keeping the remaining dough covered with the plastic wrap, roll the dough underneath your palms on the floured work surface into a long rope about ½ inch in diameter. Cut the dough into 1-inch pieces and transfer the gnocchi to the floured baking sheets. (If you wish, lightly press the tines of a fork into each piece to make ridges. This helps the gnocchi hold the sauce, but it isn't really necessary.) The gnocchi can be covered loosely with plastic wrap and refrigerated for up to 8 hours before cooking.

5. Bring a very large pot of salted water to a boil over high heat. Gradually add the gnocchi and cook until the water returns to the boil. Boil the gnocchi until they are cooked through, about 1 minute. Scoop out and reserve ½ cup of the cooking water. Carefully drain the gnocchi in a colander.

6. Transfer the gnocchi to a serving bowl. Add the pesto and mix with enough of the reserved cooking water to make a light sauce. Serve immediately, with the Parmesan passed on the side.

risotto
with peas, prosciutto, and parmesan

MAKES 4 TO 6 SERVINGS

I like to keep a bag of peas in the freezer and chopped prosciutto in the fridge so I can make this for dinner when I think that I don't have anything in the house to eat. (Of course, if you have fresh peas, just shell them and cook them in boiling water until tender.) Be sure to use Arborio or another kind of Italian risotto rice because regular long-grain rice isn't starchy enough to give the dish its milky consistency. Some cooks add heavy cream to make the "sauce," but that's cheating and adds a lot of unnecessary calories.

3 cups canned reduced-sodium chicken broth

3 cups water

4 tablespoons (½ stick) unsalted butter

⅔ cup ¼-inch-diced prosciutto

1 medium yellow onion, chopped

2 garlic cloves, minced

1½ cups Arborio or other risotto rice

1 cup dry white wine, such as Pinot Grigio

1 cup thawed frozen peas

½ cup freshly grated Parmesan cheese (2 ounces), plus more for serving

Kosher salt and freshly ground black pepper

VARIATION:
Saffron Risotto
This is the classic side dish to Osso Buco on page 107. Omit the prosciutto and peas. Add ¼ teaspoon crumbled saffron threads to the hot broth mixture.

1. Bring the stock and water to a boil in a medium saucepan over high heat. Turn the heat to very low; just enough to keep the liquid hot.

2. Heat 2 tablespoons of the butter in a large, heavy-bottomed saucepan over medium heat. Add the prosciutto and cook, stirring often, until just beginning to brown, about 2 minutes. Add the onion and garlic and cook, stirring occasionally, until the onion has softened, about 3 minutes.

3. Add the rice and cook, stirring often, until it turns from translucent to opaque (do not brown) and the rice feels heavy in the spoon, about 2 minutes. Add the wine and cook over high heat until it has evaporated to about ¼ cup, about 2 minutes.

4. Reduce the heat to medium-low. About 1 cup at a time, stir the hot stock into the rice. Cook, stirring almost constantly, until the rice absorbs almost all of the stock, about 3 minutes. Stir in another cup of stock, and stir until it is almost absorbed. Repeat, keeping the risotto at a steady simmer and adding more stock as it is absorbed, until you use all of the stock and the rice is barely tender, about 20 minutes total. (You do not have to stir the risotto constantly, and you can leave the stove occasionally for a minute or two, if necessary.) If you run out of stock and the rice isn't tender, use hot water. The risotto should have a loose consistency, one step short of soupy.

5. During the last 5 minutes of cooking, stir in the peas. Remove the risotto from the heat and stir in the remaining 2 tablespoons butter, followed by the Parmesan. Season to taste with salt and pepper. Spoon into bowls and serve hot with the additional Parmesan passed on the side.

red wine marinara sauce

MAKES 1 QUART

Every cook needs a basic meatless Italian sauce that can be used with pasta and other recipes. Marinara, named for the sailors who threw it together on their ships for quick meals, is probably the most useful. Because the sauce is usually combined with other ingredients, it should be delicious, but not overpowering. I like to use crushed tomatoes to give the marinara a smooth texture.

2 tablespoons olive oil

1 medium yellow onion, chopped

2 garlic cloves, minced

½ cup hearty red wine, such as Chianti or Shiraz

One 28-ounce can crushed tomatoes

½ cup water

2 teaspoons dried oregano

½ teaspoon freshly ground black pepper

1 bay leaf

⅔ cup coarsely chopped fresh basil

1. Heat the oil in a medium, heavy-bottomed saucepan over medium heat. Add the onion and cook, stirring occasionally, until golden, about 4 minutes. Stir in the garlic and cook until it is fragrant, about 1 minute. Add the wine and bring to a boil.

2. Stir in the tomatoes, the water, oregano, pepper, and bay leaf and bring to a simmer. Reduce the heat to medium-low and simmer, stirring occasionally, until slightly thickened, about 45 minutes. During the last 10 minutes, stir in the basil. Remove and discard the bay leaf. (The sauce can be cooled, covered, and refrigerated for up to 3 days, or frozen for up to 3 months.)

Sausage Marinara

Start by heating the oil in the saucepan over medium-high heat. Add 1 pound sweet Italian pork sausage, casings removed, and cook, stirring occasionally and breaking up the sausage into bite-size pieces with the side of a wooden spoon, until the sausage is browned, about 8 minutes. Move the sausage over to one side of the saucepan. Add the onion to the fat in the empty side of the saucepan, reduce the heat to medium, and continue as directed.

White Wine Marinara Sauce

Substitute dry white wine, such as Pinot Grigio, for the red wine.

the ultimate bolognese sauce

MAKES ABOUT 1 QUART; ENOUGH FOR 1 POUND OF PASTA (4 SERVINGS)

Bolognese is one of the glories of Italian cooking, and, despite what you may see on many restaurant menus, not just any old tomato and meat sauce. It is a commitment on the cook's part to slowly simmer such ingredients as two kinds of veal, dried porcini mushrooms, stock, wine, and a bit of tomato paste into a luscious coating for your very best pasta. I want to thank my good friend—and one of the best cooks I know—John Peca for this recipe. He uses homemade veal stock to make this extra-special sauce, but when I don't have it on hand, I use a store-bought broth, and it is still great. And it freezes perfectly, so it is a good Saturday afternoon project for making and having ready for another day.

½ ounce (about ½ cup loosely packed) dried porcini mushrooms

6 tablespoons olive oil

⅔ cup finely diced pancetta

1 garlic clove, peeled

1 small yellow onion, coarsely chopped

1 small carrot, coarsely chopped

1 small celery rib, coarsely chopped

1 pound boneless veal shoulder, cut into ½-inch cubes

1 pound ground veal

¼ cup tomato paste

½ cup dry white wine, such as Pinot Grigio

3 cups Homemade Veal Stock (page 95), store-bought veal stock, or canned reduced-sodium chicken broth

1 tablespoon finely chopped fresh basil

1 tablespoon finely chopped fresh flat-leaf parsley

1. Put the porcini in a small bowl and add enough hot tap water to cover. Allow the porcini to soften while preparing the rest of the sauce.

2. Meanwhile heat 2 tablespoons of the oil in a medium heavy-bottomed saucepan over medium heat. Add the pancetta and cook, stirring often, until lightly browned, about 3 minutes. Using a slotted spoon, transfer the pancetta to a large bowl, leaving the fat in the saucepan.

3. With the machine running, drop the garlic through the feed tube of a food processor to mince. Add the onion, carrot, and celery and pulse the processor to finely chop (but not purée) the vegetables. Add to the saucepan and cook, stirring occasionally, until the vegetables are lightly browned and leave a brown film in the saucepan, about 5 minutes. Transfer the vegetables to the bowl with the pancetta.

4. Add 2 tablespoons of the remaining oil to the saucepan and heat it over medium-high heat. Add the veal shoulder and cook, stirring occasionally with a spoon to loosen the browned vegetable juices, until the veal juices evaporate and the veal is browned, about 7 minutes. Transfer the veal shoulder to the bowl.

5. Add the remaining 2 tablespoons oil to the saucepan and heat over medium-high heat. Add the ground veal and cook, stirring occasionally with a wooden spoon to loosen the browned bits in the saucepan, until the ground veal is browned, about 7 minutes. Transfer to the bowl.

2 teaspoons finely chopped fresh thyme, or 1 teaspoon dried thyme

2 teaspoons finely chopped fresh sage, or 1 teaspoon dried sage

1 teaspoon kosher salt, plus more as needed

½ teaspoon freshly ground black pepper, plus more as needed

⅔ cup heavy cream

6. Add the tomato paste to the saucepan and cook, stirring almost constantly with a wooden spoon, until the paste coats the bottom of the saucepan with a thin, dark brown film, about 1 minute. Add the wine and bring to a boil, stirring to scrape up the browned paste. Return the veal mixture in the bowl to the saucepan.

7. Stir in the stock, basil, parsley, thyme, sage, the 1 teaspoon salt, and ½ teaspoon pepper. Bring to a boil over high heat. Reduce the heat to low and cook at a steady simmer, stirring occasionally, until the veal cubes are very tender and the liquid has reduced by about one-third, 1¾ to 2 hours. Stir in the cream, increase the heat to high and return to a simmer. Return the heat to medium-low and simmer until the liquid reduces again to make a thick, meaty sauce, about 30 minutes more. Season to taste with additional salt and pepper as needed. Use as a pasta sauce. (The sauce can be cooled, covered, and refrigerated for up to 1 day, or frozen for up to 3 months. Reheat slowly in a saucepan before serving.)

Large Pig Feet

homemade veal stock

MAKES ABOUT 2 QUARTS

You can buy chicken and beef stock fairly easily, and they are good time-savers. But veal stock is not a common item at markets yet, and it is worth making your own. Why veal and not chicken or beef broth? Because veal contains a lot of gelatin that melts into the broth, and gives the food a smooth feel in your mouth. Believe me—veal stock is the special ingredient in the dishes of many high-end Italian and French restaurants.

3 pounds veal bones

2 tablespoons vegetable oil

1 small yellow onion, chopped

1 small carrot, chopped

1 small celery stalk, chopped

6 sprigs fresh flat-leaf parsley

4 sprigs fresh thyme, or ¼ teaspoon dried thyme

8 black peppercorns

1 small bay leaf

1. Position a rack in the top third of the oven and preheat the oven to 425°F.

2. Spread the veal bones in a roasting pan. Roast, turning after 25 minutes, until the bones are deeply browned, about 45 minutes.

3. Meanwhile, heat the oil in a large stockpot over medium-high heat. Add the onion, carrot, and celery and cook, stirring occasionally, until they are beginning to brown, about 5 minutes.

4. Using tongs, transfer the roasted veal bones to the pot. Pour out the fat from the roasting pan, leaving the browned bits on the bottom of the pan. Heat the roasting pan on the stovetop over two burners on high heat until the juices are sizzling. Add about 2 cups water and bring to a boil, scraping up the browned bits in the pan with a wooden spoon. Pour this mixture into the pot. Add enough cold water (about 3 quarts) to cover the veal by 1 inch. Bring to a boil over high heat, skimming off any foam that rises to the surface. Add the parsley, thyme, peppercorns, and bay leaf. Reduce the heat to medium-low and simmer until the stock is fully flavored, 3 to 4 hours. (Do not season the stock with salt and pepper, as those seasonings will be in the recipe that uses the stock.)

5. Strain the stock through a fine-mesh sieve over a large heatproof bowl; discard the solids. Place the bowl in a larger bowl of iced water and let the stock cool to room temperature. (The stock can be transferred to covered container and refrigerated for up to 3 days, or frozen for up to 3 months.)

meats
&
poultry

braciole

MAKES 6 TO 8 SERVINGS

Braciole (pronounced "brahj-ohl") is another wonder of the Italian American kitchen where the cook makes a lot out of a little, starting with an inexpensive cut of beef and turning it into something to sing about. Making braciole is not to be taken lightly. Pounding, rolling, stuffing, tying, and braising the beef takes time, so they are reserved for special-occasion dinners. But, like all labors of love, they are worth the effort, and the exchange of flavors between the meat, filling, and sauce is something that you can't get from few minutes of sautéing. Serve these tender rolls on top of spaghetti with the sauce passed on the side.

Olive oil, for the baking dish

FILLING

1¼ cups fresh bread crumbs, made from day-old bread

⅔ cup finely diced prosciutto

⅔ cup freshly grated Pecorino Romano cheese (1½ ounces)

⅔ cup pine nuts, toasted

⅔ cup dried currants

2 tablespoons finely chopped fresh flat-leaf parsley

2 garlic cloves, minced

⅛ teaspoon freshly ground black pepper

8 top round beef steaks, cut about ¼ inch thick for braciole (about 1¼ pounds; see Note)

1 teaspoon kosher salt

½ teaspoon freshly ground black pepper

1 recipe Red Wine Marinara Sauce (page 90), heated

2 tablespoons olive oil, plus more for the baking dish

Freshly grated Pecorino Romano cheese, for serving

1. Position a rack in the center of the oven and preheat the oven to 350°F. Lightly oil a 10 by 15-inch baking dish.

2. To make the filling: Mix all of the ingredients together in a medium bowl.

3. Cut the round steaks in half vertically. One at a time, place a beef steak half between 2 self-sealing plastic bags and pound with a flat meat pounder until the meat is larger and about ¼ inch thick. For each roll, spoon a generous 2 tablespoons of the filling on a beef slice. Fold in the right and left sides by about ½ inch, then roll up from the bottom. Tie the roll into a packet with kitchen twine. Season with the salt and pepper.

4. Spread about ½ cup of the marinara sauce in the baking dish. Heat the oil in a large skillet over medium-high heat. Working in batches without crowding, add the braciole and cook, turning occasionally, until browned, about 5 minutes. Arrange the braciole, side by side, in the prepared baking dish. Pour in the remaining marinara sauce. Cover tightly with aluminum foil.

5. Bake until the braciole are tender when pierced with the tip of a small, sharp knife, about 1½ hours. Transfer the braciole to a large platter, tent with aluminum foil, and let stand for 5 minutes. Remove the twine.

6. Spoon about 1 cup of the sauce over the braciole. Pour the remaining sauce into a serving bowl. Serve hot, with the sauce and the Romano passed on the side.

Note: Butchers with Italian American clientele will carry these wide slices of top round. Otherwise, you might have to ask for them to be cut from the center of a top round roast.

chasen's chili

MAKES 12 SERVINGS

When I first came to Hollywood, Chasen's was one of the hottest restaurants in town. While it was a white-tablecloth place, it bucked conventions by serving such down-home fare as this chili. This humble dish gained international fame when Elizabeth Taylor ordered ten quarts to be delivered on dry ice to Rome when she was filming *Cleopatra*. I was very skeptical about ordering chili because I was still smarting from my first experience with Mexican food. This occurred during the filming of *The Alamo* in San Antonio, when John Wayne made fun of me because I didn't know how to eat a tamale. I eventually became a convert to Chasen's chili, and I have put away more than a piddling ten quarts over the years. Here is their classic recipe, which I have adapted to today's tastes, by adding a chopped jalapeño or two along with the bell peppers. Otherwise, one bite takes me right back to Beverly and Doheny, where Chasen's stood for almost sixty years.

8 ounces dried pinto beans, sorted over for stones, rinsed, and drained

One 28-ounce can whole tomatoes in juice, coarsely chopped, juices reserved

2 tablespoons vegetable or olive oil

1 large green bell pepper, cored, seeded, and cut into ½-inch dice

2 medium yellow onions, chopped

½ cup finely chopped fresh flat-leaf parsley

2 garlic cloves, minced

8 tablespoons (1 stick) unsalted butter, cut into tablespoon-size pieces

2 pounds coarsely ground (chili grind) beef chuck (see Notes)

1 pound coarsely ground (chili grind) boneless pork shoulder (see Notes)

⅔ cup chili powder, preferably Gebhardt's (see Notes)

1. Put the beans in a large bowl and add enough cold water to cover by 2 inches. Let the beans soak at room temperature for at least 4 and up to 8 hours. If the kitchen is hot, refrigerate them. (Or, put the beans in a large saucepan and add enough cold water to cover by 2 inches. Bring to a boil over high heat. Cook for 2 minutes. Remove from the heat, cover, and let stand for 1 hour.) Drain the beans; remove and discard the bay leaves.

2. Put the soaked beans in a large heavy-bottomed saucepan and add enough cold water to cover them by 2 inches. Bring to a boil over high heat. Reduce the heat to medium-low and simmer until just tender, about 45 minutes. Add the tomatoes and their juices and return to a simmer.

3. Heat the oil in a large skillet over medium-high heat. Add the bell pepper and cook, stirring occasionally, until softened, about 5 minutes. Add the onions and cook, stirring occasionally, until the onions are tender, about 5 minutes more. Stir in the parsley and garlic and cook until the garlic is fragrant, about 1 minute. Stir the vegetable mixture into the simmering bean mixture. Reduce the heat to medium-low. Wipe out the skillet with paper towels.

4. Melt 2 tablespoons of the butter in the skillet over medium-high heat until foamy. Mix the beef and pork together. When the foam has subsided, add one-quarter of the ground

1 tablespoon kosher salt

1½ teaspoons ground cumin

1½ teaspoons freshly ground black pepper

meats to the butter in the skillet and cook, stirring occasionally, until browned, about 5 minutes. Add the browned meat mixture to the bean mixture. Repeat three more times with the remaining butter and ground meats. Stir the chili powder, salt, cumin, and black pepper into the chili and bring to a simmer over medium-high heat, stirring often.

5. Return the heat to medium-low. Cover tightly and simmer, stirring occasionally, for 1 hour. Uncover and cook, stirring occasionally, until the liquid has reduced slightly and the meat is tender, about 30 minutes. The chili should have a loose consistency. If you like it thicker, crush some of the beans into the sauce. Skim off the fat from the surface, spoon into bowls, and serve.

Note: Some butchers sell beef chuck and pork shoulder ground for chili, which is a coarser grind than the one used for hamburger and the like. If your butcher does not, you can grind your own at home in a food processor. Cut 2 pounds each boneless beef chuck and boneless pork shoulder into 1-inch chunks and place on a baking sheet. Cover loosely with plastic wrap and freeze until the meat is partially frozen, about 2 hours. Working in batches, pulse the meat in a food processor until coarsely ground. Of course, if you have a meat grinder, fit it with the attachment with the largest holes, and put the partially frozen meat though the grinder.

Gebhardt's Chili Powder is originally from San Antonio, Texas. Its blend of ingredients is secret, but it does have a deeper flavor than other brands. Look for it in supermarkets in Texas and its surrounding states, or order it online.

osso buco

MAKES 6 SERVINGS

When Dad was a butcher, smart cooks snapped up inexpensive, but tough cuts on the bone. They knew that these cheaper meats would take extra time to cook, but that the results would be succulent and worth the wait. Now a new generation has discovered osso buco, short ribs, and the like for themselves, and the prices have jumped. For a special treat, make these braised veal shanks topped with the parsley, garlic, and lemon zest mixture called "gremolata." *Osso buco* means "bone with a hole," referring to the space in the veal bone where the marrow resides. There are many people who think that the marrow is the best part of the dish, and spread it on crusty bread or toast. The traditional side dish is the Saffron Risotto on page 89.

VEAL

Four 14- to 16-ounce cross-cut veal shanks (osso buco), cut about 1½ inches thick

2 teaspoons kosher salt, plus more as needed

1 teaspoon freshly ground black pepper, plus more as needed

4 tablespoons olive oil, plus more as needed

1 medium onion, finely chopped

1 medium carrot, cut into ½-inch dice

1 medium celery rib, cut into ½-inch dice

3 garlic cloves, minced

1 cup dry white wine, such as Pinot Grigio

One 28-ounce can whole tomatoes in juice, coarsely chopped, juices reserved

4 cups canned reduced-sodium chicken broth

2 tablespoons finely chopped fresh flat-leaf parsley

(INGREDIENTS CONTINUE)

1. Position a rack in the center of the oven and preheat the oven to 300°F.

2. To make the veal: Tie each veal shank around its "waist" and from top to bottom with kitchen twine, similar to a package. (This helps the meat stay on the bone for a nice presentation during serving. If the meal falls from the bone, don't worry, it will taste the same—delicious.) Season the veal all over with the 2 teaspoons salt and 1 teaspoon pepper.

3. Heat 2 tablespoons of the oil in a very large Dutch oven over medium-high heat. Working in batches without crowding, add the veal and cook, turning occasionally, until browned, adding more oil as needed, about 6 minutes. Transfer the veal to a plate.

4. Add the remaining 2 tablespoons oil to the pot and heat. Add the onion, carrot, celery, and garlic and reduce the heat to medium. Cover and cook, stirring occasionally, until the vegetables are almost tender, about 4 minutes. Add the wine and bring to a boil, scraping up the browned bits from the bottom of the pot with a wooden spoon. Stir in the tomatoes and their juices, the broth, parsley, rosemary, and bay leaf. Return the veal to the pot and bring to a simmer.

5. Cover the pot tightly. Braise in the oven until the veal is very tender when pierced with the tip of a small, sharp knife, about 2 hours. Transfer the veal to a platter and tent with aluminum foil to keep warm.

(RECIPE CONTINUES)

2 teaspoons finely chopped fresh rosemary, or 1 teaspoon dried rosemary

1 bay leaf

GREMOLATA

⅔ cup finely chopped fresh flat-leaf parsley

Finely grated zest of 1 lemon

2 garlic cloves, minced

6. Let the cooking liquid stand for a few minutes. Skim the fat from the surface of the cooking liquid. Bring the liquid to a boil over high heat and cook, stirring often, until reduced by about one-quarter, 10 to 15 minutes. Season the sauce to taste with salt and pepper. Remove and discard the bay leaf.

7. Meanwhile, make the gremolata: Mix the parsley, lemon zest, and garlic together in a small bowl. Cover and set aside until ready to serve.

8. For each serving, transfer a veal shank to a wide soup bowl and discard the string. Spoon the sauce around the veal, and sprinkle each shank with about a tablespoon of the gremolata. Serve hot.

veal marsala
with mushrooms

MAKES 4 SERVINGS

3 tablespoons unsalted butter

1 pound white button mushrooms, thinly sliced

1½ teaspoons kosher salt, plus more as needed

¾ teaspoon freshly ground black pepper, plus more as needed

2 tablespoons olive oil, as needed

8 large slices veal scaloppine (about 1¼ pounds)

⅔ cup all-purpose flour

⅔ cup dry Marsala wine

1½ cup canned reduced-sodium chicken broth

1. In a very large skillet over medium-high heat melt 2 tablespoons of the butter. Add the mushrooms and season them with ½ teaspoon salt and ¼ teaspoon pepper. Cook, stirring occasionally, until they are tender and lightly browned, about 10 minutes. Transfer to a bowl.

2. Season the veal on both sides with 1 teaspoon salt and ½ teaspoon pepper. Spread the flour in a shallow dish.

3. Return the skillet to medium-high heat, add the oil, and heat until the oil is hot but not smoking. In batches, to avoid crowding, coat the veal on both sides with the flour, shaking off the excess, and add to the skillet. Cook, turning once, adding more oil to the skillet as needed, until lightly browned on both sides, about 2 minutes. Transfer to a platter.

4. Return the skillet to medium-high heat. Add the Marsala and bring it to a boil, scraping up the browned bits in the bottom of the skillet with a wooden spoon. Stir in the broth and bring the mixture to a boil. Return the veal to the skillet and reduce the heat to medium. Cook at a brisk simmer, turning the veal in the skillet, until the veal is cooked through, about 2 minutes. Return to the platter. Tent the platter with aluminum foil to keep the veal warm.

5. Return the mushrooms to the skillet and increase the heat to high. Broil until the liquid is lightly thickened and reduced by about one-third, 2 to 2½ minutes. Remove from the heat. Add the remaining tablespoon butter to the skillet and stir until it melts. Season the sauce to taste with salt and pepper. Pour the mushroom sauce over the veal and serve.

veal saltimbocca

MAKES 4 SERVINGS

Veal scaloppini rolls with prosciutto and sage, *saltimbocca*, means "jump in your mouth." It is a dish that restaurant chefs love to make because each order only takes a few minutes to cook in a hot pan. At home, you probably will only be able to fit about a dozen of these little guys in your skillet, so save it for when you are making dinner for a small group.

1¾ pounds veal scaloppini

Freshly ground black pepper

4 thin slices of prosciutto, cut into 12 equal pieces to fit the veal

About 1 tablespoon finely chopped fresh sage

¼ cup all-purpose flour

3 tablespoons olive oil, plus more as needed

¾ cup dry white wine, such as Pinot Grigio

VARIATION:
Veal Saltimbocca with Fontina
Some people like to gild the lily by adding cheese to the veal before rolling them up. The cheese should be cut into sticks because slices melt too quickly and ooze out of the veal, ending up in the sauce. Cut 6 ounces of Fontina Val d'Aosta into 12 equal sticks, cut to fit the veal. Place a stick of cheese on the prosciutto, add the sage, and roll up the veal. Cook as directed above.

1. As well as you can, allowing for the size of each scaloppini, cut the veal into 12 equal pieces. One at a time, place the veal between two self-sealing plastic bags and pound with a flat meat pounder into a thin piece about 5-inches square. (Again, just do the best you can to achieve this size.)

2. Place the veal, with the grain running horizontally, on the work surface. Season with a grind or two of pepper (you will not need salt because the prosciutto and Fontina, if you add it, are both salty.) Top each piece of veal with a piece of prosciutto. Sprinkle lightly with a heaping ½ teaspoon of sage. Fold in the right and left sides by about ½ inch. Starting at the bottom, roll up the veal, and secure it with a wooden toothpick. Transfer to a plate. (The veal can be covered with plastic wrap and refrigerated for up to 4 hours.)

3. Just before serving, roll the veal in the flour to coat and shake off the excess. Heat the oil in a very large skillet over medium-high heat. Add half of the veal to the skillet and cook, turning occasionally, until browned on all sides, 4 to 5 minutes. Return to the plate. Repeat with the remaining veal, adding more oil as needed.

4. Pour out the oil from the skillet. Return it to medium-high heat and pour in the wine. Bring to a boil, scraping up the browned bits in the skillet with a wooden spoon. Add the broth and bring to a boil. Return the veal rolls to the skillet and cook over high heat, turning occasionally, until the veal shows no sign of pink when pierced with the tip of a small, sharp knife, and the sauce has thickened and reduced by about half. Transfer the veal to a platter and pour the sauce on top. Serve immediately, and remind your guests to remove the toothpicks before eating the veal.

roast pork with fig sauce

MAKES 6 TO 8 SERVINGS

Keep this recipe in mind for a special occasion—it's perfect for a Christmas main course or a Sunday dinner with company. The combination of roast pork with figs, herbs, and Port is uncomplicated and really tasty. Domestic Port will do just fine for this recipe. Black Mission figs are best because they make a dark sauce that complements the color of the pale pork. Other varieties, such as Turkish or Calimyrna, make a beige sauce that isn't as attractive.

One 2¾-pound boneless pork roast, tied crosswise with kitchen twine

1 tablespoon olive oil

2 teaspoons finely chopped fresh rosemary, or 1 teaspoon dried rosemary

2 teaspoons finely chopped fresh thyme, or 1 teaspoon dried thyme

1 teaspoon kosher salt, plus more as needed

½ teaspoon freshly ground black pepper, plus more as needed

½ cup diced dried Mission figs

¾ cup Port, such as California Tawny

2 scallions, white and pale green parts, finely chopped

¾ cup canned reduced-sodium chicken broth, plus more as needed

1. Brush the pork all over with the oil. Mix the rosemary, thyme, 1 teaspoon salt, and ½ teaspoon pepper together in a small bowl and rub the mixture into the pork. Place the pork on a roasting rack in a roasting pan and let stand at room temperature for 30 minutes.

2. Position a rack in the center of the oven and preheat the oven to 400°F.

3. Mix the figs and Port in a small bowl and set aside to soak while the pork is roasting.

4. Roast the pork for 15 minutes. Reduce the oven temperature to 350°F. Continue roasting until an instant-read thermometer inserted into the center of the roast reads 150°F, about 1 hour. Transfer the pork to a serving platter and let rest for 10 minutes.

5. Meanwhile, strain the figs in a wire sieve over a bowl, reserving the Port. Set the figs aside.

6. Pour off all but 1 tablespoon of the fat from the roasting pan. Place the pan over two burners on the stovetop on medium heat. Add the scallions to the pan and cook, stirring often, until the scallions are tender, about 1 minute. Add the reserved Port, followed by the broth, and bring to a boil over high heat, scraping up the browned bits in the pan with a wooden spoon. Boil until reduced by half, about 3 minutes.

7. Transfer the reserved figs to a blender. Add the reduced broth mixture process with the blender lid ajar, adding more broth, if needed, to make a smooth sauce. Season to taste with additional salt and pepper.

8. Remove the twine. Carve the pork crosswise into thin slices and serve with the sauce.

pork cutlets milanese on kale salad

MAKES 4 SERVINGS

Kale has made a big splash on American menus lately, but to Italians, it is an old friend. We've always had a taste for the entire family of so-called bitter greens, which also includes escarole and broccoli rabe. Here is a crisp pork cutlet served on a bed of kale salad, along with my tip for how to massage and tenderize the raw greens (the narrow-leafed lacinato variety of kale works best). The pork is also great on arugula, but in that case, skip the massage step, and just toss the greens with balsamic vinegar and olive oil, and season the salad with salt and pepper.

PORK

Four 4-ounce boneless center-cut loin pork chops

1 teaspoon kosher salt

½ teaspoon freshly ground black pepper

½ cup all-purpose flour

2 large eggs

¾ cup dried plain bread crumbs

½ cup olive oil, for frying

SALAD

20 ounces lacinato (also called Tuscan or dinosaur) kale, thick stems removed and discarded, spun dry, and torn into bite-size pieces

1 tablespoon balsamic vinegar

1 teaspoon kosher salt

3 tablespoons extra-virgin olive oil

1 cup cherry or grape tomatoes, halved

Freshly ground black pepper

Lemon wedges, for serving

1. To prepare the pork: One at a time, place a pork chop between two 1-gallon self-sealing plastic bags. Using a flat meat pounder, pound the pork to ¼-inch thickness. Season the pork cutlets with the salt and pepper.

2. Spread the flour in a shallow dish. Beat the eggs in another dish. Spread out the bread crumbs in a third dish. One at a time, coat the pork with the flour, shaking off the excess flour. Dip in the eggs, then coat with the bread crumbs, patting them on to help them adhere. Transfer to a large rimmed baking sheet. Set aside at room temperature to set the coating for at least 15 and up to 30 minutes.

3. To make the salad: Put the kale in a large bowl. Sprinkle the kale with the balsamic vinegar and salt and massage it well with your fingertips. (This breaks down the tough fibers in the kale.) Let stand for 15 minutes. Add the oil and tomatoes and toss. Season to taste with the pepper.

4. Position a rack in the center of the oven and preheat the oven to 200°F. Line a large baking sheet with a wire cake rack.

5. Heat the oil in a very large skillet over medium-high heat. Working in batches without crowding, add the pork and cook, adjusting the heat as needed, turning once, until the pork is evenly browned and shows no sign of pink when pierced in the center with the tip of a small, sharp knife, about 4 minutes. Transfer to the wire rack and keep warm in the oven while frying the remaining pork.

6. Divide the salad among four dinner plates, top each with a pork cutlet, and serve with the lemon wedges.

pork chops
with mortadella stuffing

MAKES 4 SERVINGS

Mortadella is the original bologna, having originated in the Italian city of the same name. It is much more delicious than American "baloney," and so flavorful that it can be used as a stuffing for pork chops. (I know people who even put it in their turkey dressing.) Ask for double-thick pork chops for stuffing from the butcher. These chops are great with the Roasted Potatoes with Romano and Rosemary on page 174.

Olive oil, for the baking dish

STUFFING

1½ cups fresh bread crumbs, made from day-old bread

3 tablespoons whole milk

½ cup (rind removed) finely chopped mortadella

1 tablespoon finely chopped fresh flat-leaf parsley

Kosher salt and freshly ground black pepper

1 large egg yolk

Four 12- to 14-ounce rib-eye pork chops with bone, cut about 1 inch thick

1½ teaspoons kosher salt

¾ teaspoon freshly ground black pepper

2 tablespoons olive oil

½ cup dry white wine, such as Pinot Grigio

½ cup canned reduced-sodium chicken broth

2 tablespoons tomato paste

2 teaspoons finely chopped fresh sage, or 1 teaspoon crumbled dried sage

1. Position a rack in the center of the oven and preheat the oven to 350°F. Lightly oil a 10 by 15-inch baking dish.

2. To make the stuffing: Mix the bread crumbs and milk together in a medium bowl and let stand for 3 minutes to soften the crumbs. Stir in the mortadella and parsley and season to taste with salt and pepper. Stir in the egg yolk.

3. Using a small sharp knife, cut a deep, horizontal pocket into each pork chop. Mix the salt and pepper together in a small bowl, and season the chops, inside and out, with the salt mixture. Fill each chop with an equal amount of the stuffing and close the pocket with a wooden toothpick or two.

4. Heat the oil in a large skillet over medium-high heat. Working in batches without crowding, add the chops and cook, turning once, until browned on both sides, about 5 minutes. Transfer the chops to the prepared baking dish.

5. Pour out any fat in the skillet. Return the skillet to medium-high heat and pour in the wine. Add the broth, tomato paste, and sage and bring to a boil, whisking to dissolve the paste and scraping up any browned bits in the skillet with the whisk. Pour the liquid over the chops in the baking dish and cover tightly with aluminum foil.

6. Bake until the pork shows no sign of pink when pierced at the bone with the tip of a small sharp knife, 20 to 25 minutes. (The chops are too thin to take the internal temperature with an instant-read thermometer, so the knife test works best.) For each serving, transfer each chop to a dinner plate and add a few tablespoons of the cooking liquid. Serve hot.

sausage-stuffed bell peppers

MAKES 6 SERVINGS

Stuffed bell peppers are a time-honored Italian specialty, and Mom used to make hers with standard-issue green peppers. These days, sweet red bell peppers are easily available, and they really do give better results. But you can use any color pepper you prefer, even the orange and yellow ones. In fact, if you combine different hues, this dish is good-looking enough to serve to company. Choose squat peppers that are on the small side so each one makes an individual serving, and be sure they have flat bottoms and can stand on end so they don't roll around in the dish.

FILLING

1 tablespoon olive oil, plus more for the baking dish

1 pound sweet Italian pork sausage, casings removed

2 cups fresh bread crumbs, made from day-old bread

⅔ cup whole milk

½ cup finely grated Pecorino Romano cheese (2 ounces)

1 large egg, beaten

2 tablespoons finely chopped fresh flat-leaf parsley

1 garlic clove, minced

¼ teaspoon kosher salt

¼ teaspoon freshly ground black pepper

6 sweet red bell peppers, preferably Holland peppers, about 6 ounces each

1 recipe Red Wine Marinara Sauce (page 90)

1. Position a rack in the center of the oven and preheat the oven to 375°F. Lightly oil a 10 by 15-inch baking dish.

2. To make the filling: Heat the oil in a large skillet over medium-high heat. Add the sausage meat and cook, stirring occasionally and breaking up the sausage into bite-size pieces with the side of a wooden spoon, until browned, about 8 minutes. Using a slotted spoon, transfer the sausage to a plate and let cool.

3. Put the crumbs in a medium bowl and sprinkle the milk on top. Let stand until the crumbs soften, about 3 minutes. Add the Romano, egg, parsley, garlic, salt, and black pepper and mix to combine. Stir in the sausage.

4. For each bell pepper, cut off the top (including the stem) and reserve the top. Using a dessertspoon, hollow out the pepper, discarding the ribs and seeds. Stuff the peppers with equal amounts of the filling. Return the top to each pepper. Stand the stuffed peppers in the baking dish. Pour the marinara sauce around the peppers and cover tightly with aluminum foil.

5. Bake for 30 minutes. Uncover and continue baking until the peppers are lightly charred and the filling is heated through, about 15 minutes more. Transfer each pepper and some of the sauce to deep soup bowls and serve.

sausage and spinach pie

MAKES 8 SERVINGS

From a page in Mom's recipe book, this savory pie is the kind of dish that parents still make to fill up the family for dinner. It has three surefire, crowd-pleaser ingredients that give so many dishes their Italian character—sausage, ricotta, and mozzarella. You will need a deep-dish pie plate—the filling will overflow in a standard 9-inch pan. I think of this as a macho quiche, and it is a fantastic main course for a weekend brunch.

PIE DOUGH

2 cups unbleached all-purpose flour, plus more for rolling the dough

1 teaspoon fine table salt

9 tablespoons (½ cup plus 1 tablespoon) cold vegetable shortening, cut into ½-inch cubes

3 tablespoons cold unsalted butter, cut into ½-inch cubes

⅔ cup ice-cold water, as needed

FILLING

1 tablespoon olive oil

1 pound sweet Italian pork sausage, casings removed

5 large eggs, plus 1 large egg white (reserve the yolk for the glaze)

Two 10-ounce boxes thawed frozen chopped spinach, squeezed well to remove liquid

1 pound fresh mozzarella cheese, cut into small dice

⅔ cup fresh ricotta cheese, drained

½ teaspoon kosher salt

⅛ teaspoon garlic powder

⅛ teaspoon freshly ground black pepper

1 large egg yolk (reserved from above)

1 tablespoon water

1. To make the dough: Whisk the flour and salt in a large bowl until combined. Add the shortening and butter. Using a pastry blender or two knives, rapidly cut the fats into the flour mixture until it is the consistency of coarse bread crumbs with some pea-size pieces. Be sure to retain some pea-size pieces, as they will help make the dough flaky. Gradually stir enough of the water into the flour mixture to form a dough that begins to clump together. You may not need all of the water. Gather the dough into a ball. Divide the dough in two pieces, with one piece about one-quarter larger than the other, and shape them into thick disks. Wrap each disk in plastic wrap. Refrigerate just until chilled, about 1 hour. (The dough can be refrigerated for up to 1 day. If the chilled dough is too hard to roll out, let it stand at room temperature for about 10 minutes to soften slightly.)

2. To make the filling: Heat the oil in a large skillet over medium-high heat. Add the sausage and cook, stirring occasionally and breaking up the sausage into bite-size pieces with the side of a wooden spoon, until browned, about 8 minutes. Using a slotted spoon, transfer the sausage to a plate and let cool.

3. Whisk the whole eggs and the egg white in a large bowl until blended. Add the spinach, mozzarella, ricotta, salt, garlic powder, and pepper and mix well to combine. Stir in the sausage.

4. On a lightly floured work surface, roll out the larger disk into a 14- to 15-inch round about ⅛ inch thick. Transfer to a 9½ by 1⅞-inch deep-dish pie plate. Fill the lined pie plate with the sausage mixture, letting any excess dough hang over the edges of the plate. Roll out the second disk into a 10-inch round about ⅛ inch thick. Using a pizza wheel or sharp knife

cut the dough into ¾-inch-wide strips. Arrange the strips in a crisscross pattern on the filling. Trim the overhanging dough to meet the edge of the plate. Fold the dough over and flute it, securing the ends of the strips. Freeze the pie for 15 to 20 minutes.

5. Position a rack in the bottom third of the oven and preheat the oven to 375°F.

6. Place the pie plate on a large rimmed baking sheet. Mix the reserved egg yolk with the water to make a glaze. Lightly brush some of the glaze on the top dough strips. Bake until the dough is golden brown and the filling looks slightly puffed, about 1 hour. Let cool on a wire cake rack for 10 to 15 minutes. Slice the pie and serve it warm.

frankie boys
with sausage and cheese

MAKES 8

What's a "Frankie Boy"? It's like a calzone, but with the dough shaped around the filling to make a ball. If you like baking homemade pizza, this will add a new favorite to your repertoire. Eat them hot out of the oven, or cooled to room temperature, dipped in marinara sauce or plain. They make a really great dinner accompanied by a big green salad with lots of vegetables.

"BOYS" DOUGH

¼ cup warm (105° to 115°F) water

One ¼-ounce package active dry yeast (2¼ teaspoons)

1 teaspoon sugar

1 tablespoon olive oil, plus more for the bowl

1 cup cold water

3¼ cups unbleached all-purpose flour, as needed

1½ teaspoons fine table salt

FILLING

1 tablespoon olive oil

1 pound sweet Italian pork sausage, casings removed

½ cup shredded Fontina Val d'Aosta cheese (2 ounces)

½ cup freshly grated Pecorino Romano cheese (2 ounces)

3 tablespoons Italian-seasoned dried bread crumbs

2 tablespoons finely chopped fresh flat-leaf parsley

½ teaspoon garlic powder

Olive oil, for brushing

1. To make the dough: Pour the warm water into a small bowl. Sprinkle in the yeast and sugar and let stand until the yeast softens, about 5 minutes. Stir to dissolve the yeast. Add the oil.

2. Pour the yeast mixture into a large bowl and add the cold water. Gradually stir in enough of the flour to make a stiff dough that cannot be stirred. (To make it in an electric stand mixer, mix the yeast mixture, water, oil, salt in the mixer bowl. Using the paddle attachment, with the mixer on low speed, gradually add enough flour, as necessary, to make a soft dough that cleans the sides of the bowl.)

3. Turn the dough out onto a floured work surface. Knead, adding more flour as necessary, to make a smooth, soft, and elastic dough, about 8 minutes. (Or change to the dough hook on the mixer. Knead, adding more flour as necessary, until the dough is smooth and elastic, about 8 minutes.)

4. Lightly oil a medium bowl. Shape the dough into a ball. Transfer the dough to the bowl and turn to coat with the oil. Turn the ball smooth side up and cover the bowl with plastic wrap. Let stand in a warm place until doubled in volume, about 1½ hours.

5. Meanwhile, make the filling: Heat the oil in a large skillet over medium-high heat. Add the sausage and cook, occasionally stirring and breaking up the sausage into bite-size pieces with the side of a wooden spoon, until browned, about 10 minutes. Transfer the sausage to a medium bowl and let cool. Using your fingers, crumble the sausage well. Stir in the Fontina and Romano cheeses, bread crumbs, parsley, and garlic powder.

(RECIPE CONTINUES)

6. Turn out the dough onto a work surface. Knead the dough briefly. Cut the dough into 8 equal portions, roll each into a ball, and cover loosely with plastic wrap. Working with one ball at a time, keeping the remainder covered, flatten and roll out a ball into a 6-inch-diameter round. Spoon about ½ cup of the filling into the center of the round. Bring up the edges of the round to enclose the filling, and pinch the seams well closed. Turn the ball over and shape on the work surface between cupped hands into a round shape about 3½ inches in diameter. Arrange the "boys" on a large rimmed baking sheet, spacing them well apart. Loosely cover with plastic wrap and let stand in a warm place until they look somewhat puffed but not doubled, about 45 minutes.

7. Position a rack in the center of the oven and preheat the oven to 350°F.

8. Using kitchen scissors, snip a small slit in the top of each "boy." Lightly brush the tops with oil. Bake until the "boys" are golden brown, 30 to 35 minutes. Let cool on the baking sheet for 10 minutes. Serve warm or cooled to room temperature.

mom's tripe sandwiches

MAKES 8 SANDWICHES

The cast and crew were shooting one of the *Beach Blanket* films (there were seven, plus a sequel, so I hope you'll forgive me if I don't remember which one!) on the beaches near Malibu. My folks were visiting from Philadelphia, and Mom insisted on making lunch for us. Around noon, she showed up with a brimming pot of food and made hot sandwiches for everyone. Annette Funicello (as a fellow Italian American) and I were probably the only ones who knew what she had served. When Mom was complimented on her cooking, and asked what delicacy she had prepared, she shrugged and told them, "It's only tripe." Most of the people had never had tripe …and, if given the chance, probably would have chosen meatballs. But they loved it.

Tripe is a humble food, the inner lining of the cow's stomach. It doesn't sound very promising, but cooked Mom's way, simmered in a mildly spiced tomato gravy until tender, can be melt-in-your-mouth delicious. These days, people are more adventuresome when it comes to food, and you'll find tripe (and other innards, such as kidneys and liver) on the menus of the most upscale Italian restaurants—and in the best home kitchens, too.

2 pounds honeycomb tripe

2 teaspoons kosher salt, plus more for seasoning

6 juniper berries

8 black peppercorns

3 bay leaves

1 medium carrot

6 whole cloves

2 tablespoons extra-virgin olive oil, plus more for serving

1 medium celery rib, cut into ½-inch dice

1 small yellow onion, chopped

2 garlic cloves, minced

3 cups White Wine Marinara Sauce (page 90)

2 cups water, as needed

Freshly ground black pepper

8 round crusty rolls, split and toasted

Freshly grated Romano cheese, for serving

1. Rinse the tripe very well under cold running water. Put it in a large saucepan and add enough cold water to cover by 1 inch, about 3 quarts. Bring the tripe to a boil over high heat, skimming off any foam that rises to the surface. Stir in the 2 teaspoons salt, with the juniper, peppercorns, and bay leaves. Weight the tripe with a heatproof plate or pot lid that fits inside the saucepan to keep the tripe submerged in the cooking liquid. Reduce the heat to low and partially cover the saucepan. Simmer, adding hot water to the saucepan to keep the tripe covered, if needed, and stirring occasionally to prevent sticking to the bottom, until the tripe is barely tender and not mushy, 2 to 2 ½ hours. Drain the tripe and discard the spices. Let the tripe cool.

2. Meanwhile, cut a 1-inch chunk from the top end of the carrot. Pierce the clove in six places with the tip of a knife, and insert a clove into each slit; set the carrot chunk aside. (You could just add the cloves to the sauce, but the chunk will be easier to find and discard with the hard cloves before serving.) Cut the remaining carrot into ½-inch dice.

3. Heat the oil in a large skillet over medium heat. Add the chopped carrot, the carrot chunk with cloves, celery, and onion, and cook, stirring occasionally, until the onion is softened, about 3 minutes. Stir in the garlic and cook until it is fragrant, about 1 minute. Stir in the marinara sauce and 1 cup of the water. Bring the sauce to a simmer. Reduce the heat to low and simmer gently for 15 minutes.

4. Cut the tripe across the grain (look closely on the smooth side of the tripe, and you'll see it) into strips about 2 inches long and ½ inch wide. Stir the tripe into saucepan, and stir in the remaining water, plus more as needed, to cover the tripe with the sauce. Return to a simmer over high heat. Reduce the heat to medium-low and simmer, stirring occasionally and adding more hot water as needed if the sauce becomes too thick, until the tripe is tender but slightly chewy, about 45 minutes. Discard the carrot chunk with the cloves. Season to taste with salt and pepper.

5. Fill each roll with the stewed tripe, sprinkle with Romano, and drizzle with olive oil. Serve hot on plates with forks and knives.

roman lamb sauté
with white wine and herbs

When I first went to Rome in the early sixties to film a television special, it was the time of director Federico Fellini's heyday. Day-to-day life seemed to be a replica of his movie about the Roman social world, *La Dolce Vita,* when the most important thing was being seen at the best tables at the most popular outdoor cafés. You could hardly hear conversation because of the motor scooters zipping by, and I spent a lot of time smiling at the *paparazzi* that swarmed everywhere in packs, taking pictures of the celebrities that were in town for various reasons. It was a new and fun experience for me, totally different from anything in America, even in the big cities. This Roman specialty, *abbacchio alla cacciatora* (hunter-style lamb), reminds me of those times. Usually a long-simmered stew of young spring lamb, its fragrance is almost intoxicating with herbs, wine, and a piquant aroma from wine vinegar. Here it is made quickly with boneless leg of lamb. It should be served with a side of polenta, rice, or orzo to catch the sauce.

2 tablespoons olive oil, plus more as needed

2¾ pounds boneless leg of lamb, trimmed of fat and sinew, cut into 1½-inch cubes (about 2 pounds after trimming)

2 garlic cloves, thinly sliced

1 teaspoon anchovy paste

1 tablespoon finely chopped fresh rosemary, or 1½ teaspoons crumbled dried rosemary

1 teaspoon finely chopped fresh sage, or 1½ teaspoon crumbled dried sage

¼ teaspoon hot red pepper flakes

2 teaspoons all-purpose flour

½ cup dry white wine, such as Pinot Grigio

¼ cup white or red wine vinegar

Kosher salt

1. Heat 1 tablespoon of the oil in a very large skillet over high heat. Working in batches without crowding, cook the lamb, turning occasionally, until browned on all sides but still red when pierced in the center with the tip of a small, sharp knife, about 5 minutes, adding more oil as needed. Transfer to a plate.

2. Add the remaining 1 tablespoon oil to the skillet and heat. Add the garlic and anchovy paste and cook, stirring often, until the garlic has softened, about 1 minute. Return the lamb and its juices to the pan, and stir in the rosemary, sage, and red pepper flakes. Cook until the juices have reduced to a glaze, about 1 minute. Sprinkle with the flour and mix in well.

3. Add the wine and vinegar and bring to a boil, scraping up the browned bits on the bottom of the skillet. Reduce the heat to medium and simmer until the sauce thickens slightly and the lamb is reheated and pink when pierced into the center with the knife, 1 to 2 minutes for medium rare Season to taste with salt. Serve hot.

roast chicken
with chestnut-sausage stuffing

MAKES 6 SERVINGS

Is there any kitchen aroma more comforting than a chicken cooking in the oven? It's best to cook a large roasting chicken so you have a large carcass for making stock and soup, and the possibility of leftover meat. Also, if you like stuffing as much as I do (especially this one with Italian flavors like sausage, Romano, and chestnuts), then the larger chicken allows you to fill it up more. You can never fit all of the stuffing in the bird, so expect to bake some on the side as well. This recipe has a bunch of little tricks to produce a juicy bird with golden brown skin.

CHICKEN

One 7½-pound roasting chicken, giblets reserved for another use (save them for Next-Day Chicken Stock on page 40)

2 teaspoons kosher salt

1 teaspoon freshly ground black pepper

STUFFING

1 tablespoon olive oil, plus more for the baking dish

10 ounces sweet Italian pork sausages, casings removed (about 3 links)

½ cup chopped yellow onion

2 medium celery ribs, cut into ½-inch dice

3 cups soft bread crumbs, made from day-old bread

One 3½-ounce package vacuum-packed cooked chestnuts (see Note), coarsely chopped (about ¾ cup)

½ cup freshly grated Pecorino Romano cheese (2 ounces)

2 tablespoons finely chopped fresh flat-leaf parsley

(INGREDIENTS CONTINUE)

1. To prepare the chicken: At least 8 hours before cooking the chicken, pull out any fat from the tail area. (If the butcher has already removed the fat, skip it.) Cover and refrigerate the fat until ready to roast the chicken. Sprinkle the chicken inside and out with the salt and pepper. Place the chicken on a wire rack in a baking sheet and refrigerate, uncovered, for at least 8 and up to 24 hours.

2. Just before roasting the chicken, make the stuffing: Heat the oil in a large skillet over medium-high heat. Add the sausage and cook, stirring occasionally and breaking it up into bite-size pieces with a wooden spoon, until it is lightly browned and has lost its raw look, about 8 minutes. Using a slotted spoon, transfer the sausage to a bowl, leaving the fat in the skillet.

3. Add the onion and celery to the skillet and reduce the heat to medium. Cover and cook, stirring occasionally, until the vegetables are tender, about 10 minutes. Add the vegetable mixture to the sausage. Add the crumbs, chestnuts, Romano, parsley, rosemary, and sage. Stir in enough of the broth to moisten the stuffing, about ½ cup. Season lightly to taste with salt and pepper.

4. Position a rack in the center of the oven and preheat the oven to 400°F.

5. Loosely stuff some of the warm stuffing into the chicken. Cover the exposed stuffing with a small piece of aluminum foil. Transfer the remaining stuffing to a small oiled baking dish

(RECIPE CONTINUES)

2 teaspoon finely chopped fresh rosemary, or 1 teaspoon dried rosemary

2 teaspoons finely chopped fresh sage, or 1 teaspoon crumbled dried sage

½ cup canned reduced-sodium chicken broth, plus more as needed

Kosher salt and freshly ground black pepper

Olive oil, for rubbing the chicken

¼ cup dry white wine, such as Pinot Grigio

1 cup canned reduced-sodium chicken broth

(any size or shape large enough to hold the stuffing in a layer about 1 inch thick will do), cover it with aluminum foil, and refrigerate until ready to reheat it.

6. Tuck the wing tips behind the chicken shoulders. Tie the drumstick together with a piece of kitchen twine or unwaxed dental floss. (Yes, it works.) Rub the chicken all over with the oil. Place the chicken, breast side down, on a V-shaped roasting rack in a roasting pan. Add the reserved chicken fat to the pan, if you have it.

7. Roast for 30 minutes. Turn the chicken breast side up and continue roasting, basting every 20 minutes or so with the fat in the pan, until an instant-read thermometer inserted in the thickest part of the thigh and not touching a bone reads 170°F, about 1¼ hours. During the last 10 minutes or so, add the stuffing in the baking dish to the oven. Remove the chicken from the oven and let rest at room temperature for 15 minutes. Reduce the oven temperature to 350°F and continue baking the stuffing in the dish until it is heated through, about 15 minutes. (If you like crusty stuffing, remove the foil.)

8. Tilt the roasting pan and skim off any fat from the pan juices. Heat the roasting pan over high heat on the stovetop until the pan juices are sizzling. Add the wine, followed by the stock, and bring to a boil, scraping up the browned bits in the pan with a wooden spoon. Boil, stirring often, until the mixture has reduced to about ⅔ cup, about 3 minutes. Remove from the heat.

9. Spoon the stuffing out of the chicken and add to the baking dish with the other stuffing. Carve the chicken and arrange the meat on a serving platter. Drizzle with the pan juices and serve immediately with the stuffing.

Note: Cooked chestnuts are now available at specialty markets (especially Asian grocers) and many supermarkets in vacuum-sealed bags. You may also find the cooked chestnuts packed in 1-pound jars, but the smaller bags are convenient and less expensive.

chicken cacciatore

MAKES 4 SERVINGS

One of the all-time great Italian American comfort foods, chicken cacciatore should always have a lot of mushrooms in the sauce. (*Cacciatore* means "hunter-style," and the hunter would have foraged for wild mushrooms for cooking this dish.) Because chicken breast cooks more quickly than the dark meat, watch out for overcooking, and take them out of the sauce a few minutes before the other pieces.

One 4-pound chicken, cut into 8 serving pieces

Kosher salt and freshly ground black pepper

½ cup all-purpose flour

4 tablespoons olive oil, plus more as needed

10 ounces cremini or white mushrooms, thinly sliced

1 medium red bell pepper, cored, seeded, and chopped

1 medium yellow onion, chopped

2 garlic cloves, minced

1 teaspoon dried oregano

1 teaspoon finely chopped fresh rosemary, or ½ teaspoon dried rosemary

One 28-ounce can crushed tomatoes

½ cup dry white wine, such as Pinot Grigio

Chopped fresh flat-leaf parsley, for serving (optional)

1. Season the chicken with salt and pepper. In a medium bowl, toss the chicken with the flour to coat and shake off the excess flour.

2. Heat 2 tablespoons of the oil in a large skillet over medium-high heat. Working in batches, add the chicken and cook, turning occasionally, adding more oil as needed, until the chicken is browned, about 6 minutes. Transfer the chicken to a plate. Wipe out the skillet.

3. Return the skillet to medium heat. Add the remaining 2 tablespoons oil and heat. Add the mushrooms, bell pepper, and garlic and cook, stirring occasionally, until the mushrooms are beginning to brown, about 10 minutes. During the last minute, stir in the garlic, oregano, and rosemary. Stir in the tomatoes and wine and bring to a boil..

4. Return the chicken to the skillet and reduce the heat to medium-low. Cover tightly and simmer until the breast halves show no sign of pink when pierced in the thickest part with the tip of a small, sharp knife, about 35 minutes. Transfer the breast halves to a platter and tent with aluminum foil to keep warm. Keep cooking the thighs, drumsticks, and wings until the thighs show no sign of pink when pierced at the bone with the tip of the knife, about 10 minutes more. Return the breasts to the skillet and reheat them, about 2 minutes.

5. Transfer the chicken to a platter, sprinkle with the parsley, if using, and serve.

pan-roasted chicken breast
with rosemary and lemon sauce

MAKES 4 SERVINGS

Whenever I am on the road, I gravitate to Italian restaurants for some comfort food to remind me of home. Lemon chicken can come in many forms, and you'll often see it on menus as a sautéed boneless chicken cutlet with lemon sauce. But this is a soulful roasted version, with crisp skin and a tart, brown sauce. Serve Roasted Potatoes with Romano and Rosemary on page 174 alongside.

3 large lemons

1 tablespoon extra-virgin olive oil

Four 8- to 10-ounce skin-on, bone-in chicken breasts

1 teaspoon kosher salt

½ teaspoon freshly ground black pepper

½ cup canned reduced-sodium chicken broth

1½ teaspoons finely chopped fresh rosemary, or ¾ teaspoon crumbled dried rosemary, plus more chopped fresh rosemary, for garnish

1 teaspoon cornstarch

1 garlic clove, minced

1. Position a rack in the top third of the oven and preheat the oven to 400°F.

2. Slice 1 lemon into ¼-inch rounds. Finely grate the zest from another lemon. Squeeze the juice from the 2 whole lemons; you should have ⅔ cup.

3. Heat the oil in a large ovenproof skillet over medium-high heat. Season the chicken breasts all over with the salt and pepper. Working in batches, add the chicken to the oil, skin side down. Cook until the skin is well browned, about 4 minutes. Turn and cook the other side until lightly browned, about 2 minutes. Transfer the browned chicken to a platter.

4. Pour off all but 2 tablespoons of the fat from the skillet. Return the chicken to the skillet and top with the lemon slices. Bake, basting occasionally with the pan juices, until an instant-read thermometer inserted in the thickest part of the chicken reads 170°F, about 35 minutes. Transfer the chicken with the lemon slices to a deep serving platter.

5. Mix the lemon juice and zest with the broth and 1½ teaspoons rosemary in a small bowl. Sprinkle the cornstarch into the mixture and stir to dissolve. Return the skillet to medium heat. Add the garlic and cook, stirring often, until the garlic is beginning to color, about 1 minute. Add the cornstarch mixture and cook, scraping up the browned bits from the bottom of the skillet, until the sauce is boiling and lightly thickened.

6. Pour the sauce over the chicken, sprinkle with the additional rosemary, and serve immediately.

chicken thighs
with peas, sweet vermouth, and sherry

MAKES 4 SERVINGS

This dish of meaty chicken thighs baked in an aromatic sauce is one of my specialties, and I can make it with my eyes closed (do not try that at home!) It has only been recently that people drink enough wine at home to cook with it, but every Italian family in South Philly had a bottle of sherry or vermouth tucked away. Be sure to serve the chicken with rice or orzo to soak up the sauce.

8 skin-on, bone-in chicken thighs (see Note)

1½ teaspoons kosher salt, plus more as needed

¾ teaspoon freshly ground black pepper, plus more as needed

2 tablespoons olive oil

1 medium yellow onion, chopped

2 garlic cloves, minced

½ cup dry sherry

½ cup sweet vermouth

2 tablespoons cornstarch

2 tablespoons cold water

1 cup thawed frozen peas

1. Position a rack in the center of the oven and preheat the oven to 350°F. Lightly oil a 9 by 13-inch baking dish.

2. Season the chicken all over with the salt and pepper. Heat the oil in a large skillet over medium-high heat. Working in batches without crowding, add the chicken, skin side down, to the skillet and cook until the underside is golden brown, about 5 minutes. Flip the chicken over and brown the other side of the chicken, about 2 minutes more. Transfer the chicken to the baking dish.

3. Pour off all but 2 tablespoons of the fat from the skillet. Add the onion and reduce the heat to medium. Cook, stirring often, until the onion has softened, about 3 minutes. Stir in the garlic and cook until fragrant, about 1 minute. Add the sherry and vermouth and bring to a boil, scraping up the browned bits in the skillet with a wooden spoon. Pour the mixture over the chicken.

4. Bake until the chicken shows no sign of pink when pierced at the bone with the tip of a small, sharp knife, about 45 minutes. Remove the baking dish from the oven.

5. Sprinkle the cornstarch over the 2 tablespoons cold water in a small bowl and stir to dissolve the cornstarch. Stir the cornstarch mixture into the cooking juices in the baking dish, and scatter the peas on top of the chicken. Return to the oven and bake until the sauce is simmering and thickened and the peas are heated through, 5 to 10 minutes. Season the sauce to taste with additional salt and pepper as needed, and serve.

Note: If you prefer, substitute boneless, skinless chicken thighs, and cook them for about 35 minutes before adding the peas and dissolved cornstarch.

seafood

WHOLE ROASTED BRANZINO WITH FENNEL AND PANCETTA 142

SEA BASS WITH HORSERADISH BREAD CRUMBS 143

SNAPPER IN ACQUA PAZZA 145

SWORDFISH KEBABS
WITH LEMON AND BASIL MARINADE 146

SHRIMP SCAMPI 149

CLAMS FRA DIAVOLO 150

STUFFED CALAMARI 151

SEAFOOD SALAD WITH LEMON DRESSING 154

whole roasted branzino
with fennel and pancetta

MAKES 2 SERVINGS

Branzino deserves its reputation as being one of the most delicious of all fish. Popular all over the Mediterranean, it is now common to find it imported here. But, most of the fish are the small side and not easy to fillet, so it's best to roast them whole and then remove the cooked flesh from the bone. I cook the fish on a bed of chopped fennel and pancetta, and the exchange of flavors is fantastic. You can easily double the recipe for four people, dividing the fish and fennel mixture between two baking dishes.

FENNEL AND PANCETTA

1 large fennel bulb, about 14 ounces

1 tablespoon olive oil, plus more for the baking dish and fish

⅔ cup diced pancetta

Kosher salt and freshly ground black pepper

Two 14- to 16-ounce branzini, cleaned and scaled

½ teaspoon kosher salt

½ teaspoon freshly ground black pepper

Lemon wedges, for serving

1. Position a rack in the top third of the oven and preheat the oven to 400°F. Lightly oil a 10 by 15-inch baking dish.

2. To prepare the fennel and pancetta: Trim and core the fennel. Chop the fronds and reserve them in a small bowl for serving. Chop the bulbs and stalks into a ½-inch dice. Heat the oil in a large skillet over medium heat. Add the pancetta and cook, stirring often, until it is lightly browned, about 3 minutes. Using a slotted spoon, transfer the pancetta to paper towels to drain, leaving the fat in the skillet.

3. Add the diced fennel to the skillet and cook, stirring occasionally, until crisp-tender. Stir in the pancetta and season to taste with some salt and pepper. Spread the fennel mixture in the baking dish.

4. Using a sharp knife, cut 3 diagonal, parallel slits about ¼ inch deep into the meaty part on both sides of each fish, spacing the cuts about 1 inch apart. Lightly brush the fish all over with the oil and season with the ½ teaspoon salt and ½ teaspoon pepper. Arrange the fish on the bed of fennel in the baking dish.

5. Bake, uncovered, until the fish in one of the slits is opaque when flaked to the bone with the tip of a small, sharp knife, about 20 minutes.

6. To serve, using the knife, cut down the backbone of one fish. Using a soup spoon as an aide, loosen the fish fillet from the bones and transfer to a dinner plate. Starting at the tail, lift off and discard the bones and head. Transfer the remaining fillet to the plate. Repeat with the remaining fish. Sprinkle the fillets with the chopped fronds and serve with the lemon wedges.

sea bass
with horseradish bread crumbs

Italians love seafood, as they are blessed with a few thousand miles of coastline, and many Italian Americans come from regions that subsisted on fish. Horseradish (*rafano*) is not a common Italian ingredient, and it is usually served with beef. My good buddy John Peca taught me this recipe, and an easier (and classier) main seafood main course would be hard to find. Use a thick and meaty fish, such as Chilean sea bass or halibut, so the crumbs have time to brown in the oven while the fish bakes.

Olive oil, for the baking dish

Four 6-ounce Chilean sea bass fillets, skin removed, about 1½ inches thick

1 teaspoon kosher salt

4 teaspoons thick and creamy store-bought horseradish sauce (see Note)

½ cup fresh bread crumbs, made from day-old bread

Finely chopped fresh flat-leaf parsley, for garnish

Lemon wedges, for serving

1. Position a rack in the top third of the oven and preheat the oven to 350°F. Lightly oil a 9 by 13-inch baking dish.

2. Season the fish all over with the salt. Spread the top (not the skinned side) of each fillet with the horseradish sauce. Spread the bread crumbs in a plate. Dip each fillet, sauced side down, into the crumbs, and pat the crumbs to help them adhere. Arrange the fillets in the dish.

3. Bake until the crumbs are lightly browned and the fish is opaque when pierced into the center with the tip of a small, sharp knife, about 20 minutes. Let stand for 3 minutes. Sprinkle with the parsley and serve hot, with the lemon wedges.

Note: Look for this sauce in small jars in the condiment aisle of the supermarket. Do not use refrigerated prepared horseradish, which is too coarse.

snapper in acqua pazza

MAKES 4 SERVINGS

Fish cooked *all' acqua pazza* means that it is simmered in a flavor-packed "crazy water." I don't know if crazy is the right way to describe this spicy broth, but it sure is good. There are many versions out there, and you can make substitutions, as you wish. A teaspoon of fresh rosemary could stand in for the basil, or you could use green olives instead of the black ones. Snapper works well, but there's no reason that you couldn't try another mild fish, such as grouper or mahi-mahi.

2 tablespoons extra-virgin olive oil

2 scallions, white and green parts, finely chopped

1 garlic clove, minced

½ cup dry white wine, such as Pinot Grigio

½ cup water

2 tablespoons fresh lemon juice

½ teaspoon hot red pepper flakes

12 ounces cherry tomatoes, halved

⅔ cup coarsely chopped pitted kalamata olives

2 tablespoons finely chopped fresh basil or flat-leaf parsley, plus more for garnish

¼ teaspoon kosher salt, plus more as needed

Freshly ground black pepper

Four 6-ounce red snapper fillets, with skin

1. Heat the oil in a large, deep skillet over medium heat. Add the scallions and garlic and cook, stirring often, until they are tender, about 2 minutes. Stir in the wine, ½ cup water, lemon juice, red pepper flakes, and ¼ teaspoon of the salt and bring to a simmer. Reduce the heat to low, partially cover the skillet, and simmer to blend the flavors, about 10 minutes.

2. Add the cherry tomatoes, olives, and the 2 tablespoons basil and return the liquid to a simmer. Arrange the fillets on top of the mixture and cover. Simmer until the fish is opaque when flaked in the thickest part with the tip of a small, sharp knife, 8 to 10 minutes. Season the cooking liquid to taste with salt and black pepper.

3. For each serving, transfer a fillet to a shallow serving bowl and top with one-quarter of the tomato mixture with its broth. Sprinkle with the additional basil and serve.

swordfish kebabs
with lemon and basil marinade

MAKES 6 SERVINGS

When the weather cooperates (which, I have to admit, is pretty often in Los Angeles), my sons and sons-in-law usually take over at the grill and I sit back in the sun and enjoy being with my family. The beauty of this dish is that it is so easy to make, and doesn't take a lot of concentration to feed a crowd. The meaty flavor of the swordfish can stand up to the lemon and basil. But don't overmarinate the fish, or the acid can "cook" it and change the texture.

MARINADE

¼ cup extra-virgin olive oil

¼ cup dry white wine, such as Pinot Grigio

Finely grated zest of 1 lemon

2 tablespoons fresh lemon juice

2 teaspoons Dijon mustard

½ teaspoon kosher salt

¼ teaspoon hot red pepper flakes

2 tablespoons coarsely chopped fresh basil

2 pounds swordfish, cut 1 inch thick, skin removed

1 large red bell pepper, cored, seeded, and cut into 24 pieces about 1½ inches square

Olive oil, for brushing

6 long metal grilling skewers (or use long bamboo skewers, soaked in water for 30 minutes)

Lemon wedges, for serving

1. To make the marinade: In a blender, process the oil, wine, lemon zest and juice, mustard, salt, and red pepper flakes until thickened. Add the basil and pulse until it is minced. Pour the marinade into a 1-gallon, self-sealing plastic bag. Cut the swordfish into 1½-inch chunks. Add the swordfish to the marinade, close the bag, and refrigerate, turning occasionally, for 30 minutes to 1 hour, no longer.

2. Prepare an outdoor grill for direct cooking over medium-high heat (450°F).

3. For each kebab, thread 4 swordfish chunks alternating with 4 red bell pepper pieces, onto a skewer. (If using bamboo skewers, wrap the exposed end of the skewer in aluminum foil to help keep it from burning.) Lightly brush the kebabs all over with the oil.

4. Brush the grill grate clean. Grill the kebabs, with the lid closed as much as possible, turning once or twice, until the swordfish is just opaque when pierced at the center, about 8 minutes. Transfer to a platter. Serve hot, with the lemon wedges.

shrimp scampi

MAKES 4 SERVINGS

One of the quickest seafood entrées to cook, shrimp scampi is a real crowd-pleaser, and can easily be adapted to your personal taste. If you like more garlic or lemon, go for it, and I won't stop you if you want to substitute basil for the parsley. My recipe makes plenty of sauce for serving the scampi over linguine or sopping up with focaccia.

2 tablespoons olive oil

2 garlic cloves, thinly sliced

1½ pounds jumbo shrimp (21–25 count), peeled and deveined

½ cup dry white wine, such as Pinot Grigio, or dry vermouth

Finely grated zest of 1 lemon

2 tablespoons fresh lemon juice

¼ teaspoon hot red pepper flakes

2 tablespoons cold unsalted butter, cut into ½-inch cubes

Kosher salt

2 tablespoons finely chopped fresh flat-leaf parsley

1. Heat the oil and garlic together in a large skillet over medium-high heat, stirring often, just until the garlic starts to turn golden brown, about 1 minute. Add the shrimp and cook, stirring occasionally, just until the shrimp are opaque on the outside, about 3 minutes.

2. Add the wine, lemon zest and juice, and red pepper flakes. Bring the mixture to a full boil, stirring often. Using a slotted spoon, transfer the shrimp to a platter. Off the heat, add the butter and stir until it has melted and slightly thickened the sauce. Season to taste with the salt. Stir in the parsley. Return the shrimp to the sauce and serve.

clams fra diavolo

Fra Diavolo translates to the "Brother Devil" of lore, a demon who would naturally season his tomato sauce with hellishly hot dried chilies. When I make these clams in the spicy sauce, I keep it on the "not *too* hot" side, because you can always add more chilies, but you can't take them out. Serve these over plain linguine or just with some crusty bread. Another time, try it with mussels.

....

4 dozen littleneck clams, scrubbed well under cold running water

SAUCE

2 tablespoons olive oil

1 medium yellow onion, chopped

3 garlic cloves, minced

1 teaspoon hot red pepper flakes

½ cup dry white wine, such as Pinot Grigio

One 28-ounce can crushed tomatoes

½ cup water

2 tablespoons chopped fresh flat-leaf parsley, plus more for serving

2 teaspoons dried oregano

½ teaspoon freshly ground black pepper

1 bay leaf

1. Soak the clams in a large bowl of salted iced water for about 1 hour.

2. Meanwhile, make the sauce: Heat the oil in a large heavy-bottomed saucepan over medium heat. Add the onion and cook, stirring occasionally, until golden, about 4 minutes. Stir in the garlic and red pepper flakes and cook until the garlic is fragrant, about 1 minute. Add the wine and bring to a boil. Stir in the tomatoes, water, the 2 tablespoons of parsley, the oregano, black pepper, and bay leaf and bring to a simmer. Reduce the heat to medium-low and simmer, stirring occasionally, until lightly thickened, about 45 minutes. Remove and discard the bay leaf.

3. Drain the clams and rinse well under cold running water. Add the clams to the simmering sauce and tightly cover the saucepan. Cook, occasionally shaking the saucepan, until all of the clams open, 8 to 10 minutes. Discard any clams that do not open.

4. Divide the clams and sauce evenly among four deep bowls. Sprinkle with the remaining parsley and serve immediately.

stuffed calamari

In most Italian American households, dinner on Christmas Eve is always "The Feast of the Seven Fishes," an all-seafood meal with a parade of seven or more fish specialties. Stuffed calamari is one of the most anticipated of them all. This recipe makes a dozen stuffed squid, an amount easily multiplied depending on the other items on your menu. They are often served on linguine, in which case, cook the calamari with 4 cups (1 recipe) of the marinara sauce.

12 calamari bodies, with tentacles, cleaned

2 cups plain dried bread crumbs

⅔ cup freshly grated Pecorino Romano cheese (1½ ounces)

2 tablespoons finely chopped fresh flat-leaf parsley

2 garlic cloves, minced

Kosher salt and freshly ground black pepper

1 large egg, beaten

Olive oil, for the baking dish

2 cups White Wine Marinara Sauce (page 90), cooled

1. Pulse the calamari tentacles in a food processor until very finely chopped but not a paste. (Or chop them with a heavy knife.) Add the bread crumbs, Romano, parsley, and garlic. Season to taste with salt and pepper. Add the egg and mix until moistened.

2. Lightly oil a 9 by 13-inch baking dish. Spread the bottom with about ½ cup of the marinara sauce.

3. Using your fingers, loosely fill each calamari body with the bread crumb mixture, making sure not to pack the stuffing in and leaving about ½ inch at the top. (The stuffing will expand during cooking.) Close the top of the each body with a wooden toothpick, and arrange, side by side, in the prepared baking dish. Top with the remaining sauce. Cover tightly with aluminum foil. (The calamari can be refrigerated at this point for up to 12 hours.)

4. Position a rack in the center of the oven and preheat the oven to 350°F. Bake the stuffed calamari until the sauce is bubbling in the middle of the dish and the calamari are tender, 45 to 55 minutes. Serve hot.

seafood salad
with lemon dressing

MAKES 6 TO 8 SERVINGS

This is another dish that you will find gracing millions of tables on Christmas Eve. There are a few tips to making it perfectly. Take the time to cook each seafood component separately—they each only take a few minutes, so you aren't going to save any time by cooking them together. And don't overcook the seafood, because the lemon juice is going to "cook" it. Some cooks add sliced scungilli (also called conch). If you want to do this, I have to warn you that the fresh kind is very tough. Take my advice and use the canned version, and don't cook it yourself unless you have a couple of hours to spare.

2 pounds cultivated mussels (see Note), scrubbed under cold running water

½ cup dry white wine, such as Pinot Grigio

½ small yellow onion, finely chopped

12 ounces calamari bodies, tentacles optional

2 cups water

2 pounds extra-large (26–30 count) shrimp, peeled and deveined

1 pound sea scallops

3 tablespoons fresh lemon juice

⅔ cup extra-virgin olive oil

3 medium celery ribs, thinly sliced

2 scallions, white and green parts, thinly sliced

⅔ cup drained and sliced pimiento-stuffed green olives

3 tablespoons finely chopped fresh flat-leaf parsley

½ teaspoon kosher salt, plus more as needed

¼ teaspoon freshly ground black pepper, plus more as needed

1. Put the mussels, wine, and onion in a large saucepan and cover. Cook over high heat, occasionally shaking the saucepan, until all of the mussels have opened, 5 to 10 minutes. Using tongs, transfer the mussels to a large bowl; discard any unopened mussels. Strain the cooking liquid through a fine-mesh wire sieve into a small bowl, leaving any grit behind in the saucepan. Rinse the saucepan.

2. Return the strained cooking liquid to the saucepan and add the water. Bring to a boil over high heat. Add the calamari (including the tentacles, if using), return to a boil, and cook just until the calamari is opaque, about 1 minute. Using a wire spider or slotted spoon, transfer the calamari to the bowl with the mussels, leaving the liquid in the saucepan.

3. Add the shrimp to the saucepan and cook just until they turn opaque, about 3 minutes. Using the spider, transfer the shrimp to the bowl, leaving the liquid in the saucepan.

4. Add the scallops to the saucepan and cook just until they turn opaque, about 3 minutes. Drain the scallops and add them to the bowl. Let the seafood cool.

5. Remove the mussels from the shells, reserving about a dozen mussels in the shell for garnish. Cut the calamari bodies into ⅛-inch rings, and coarsely chop the tentacles, if using. Cut the scallops into ¼-inch rounds. Mix the mussels, calamari, shrimp, and scallops together in a large serving bowl.

(RECIPE CONTINUES)

6. Whisk the lemon juice, the ½ teaspoon salt, and ¼ teaspoon pepper together in a small bowl. Gradually whisk in the oil. Pour the dressing over the seafood mixture, add the celery, scallions, green olives, and parsley, and mix well. Cover and refrigerate until chilled, at least 2 hours and up to 1 day. Season to taste with additional salt and pepper and serve chilled.

Note: Cultivated mussels are a lot easier to clean than wild ones—just give them a good scrub under cold running water, and that's it. If using wild mussels, scrub them, soak in salted ice water for 1 to 2 hours, then drain. Using pliers, pull off any of the fuzzy cords (beards) extruding from the mussels, and cook as directed.

vegetables & sides

roasted broccolini
with olives

You might think that broccolini is miniature broccoli, but it actually is a Japanese hybrid of Chinese broccoli. Regardless of its heritage, it can easily pick up Italian flavors. Roasting has become a new way to cook vegetables that you would normally boil. In addition to adding flavor, roasting is healthy because it doesn't leave the nutrients behind in the water. This side dish is especially tasty with salmon.

Two 10-ounce bunches broccolini

3 tablespoons olive oil, plus more for the baking sheet

⅔ cup coarsely chopped pitted kalamata olive

1 garlic clove, finely chopped

⅛ teaspoon hot red pepper flakes

Kosher salt

1. Position a rack in the top third of the oven and preheat the oven to 400°F. Lightly oil a large rimmed baking sheet.

2. Rinse the broccolini well, but do not dry it. Place it on the prepared baking sheet and toss with 2 tablespoons of the oil. Arrange the broccolini in a single layer. Roast, flipping the broccolini halfway through the cooking, until the broccolini is crisp-tender and beginning to brown, about 15 minutes.

3. Mix the olives, garlic, red pepper flakes, and the remaining 1 tablespoon oil together in a small bowl. Stir the olive mixture into the broccolini and continue roasting until the garlic is fragrant, about 3 minutes more. Season to taste with salt and serve.

escarole
with pancetta and garlic

MAKES 6 SERVINGS

If you come from Italian stock, then there is a 99 percent chance that you know and love escarole. This leafy green has lots of flavor, but it can be on the bitter side. Here the pancetta and garlic smooth out its rough edges, as it were. I also give a variation for broccoli rabe, too, another beloved Italian green, which can be cooked the same way.

2 heads escarole, about 10 ounces each, coarsely chopped

2 tablespoons olive oil

⅔ cup diced pancetta

2 garlic cloves, finely chopped

Kosher salt and freshly ground black pepper

1. Escarole is always sandy, and needs to be washed well. Put the chopped escarole in a sink or large bowl of cold water and agitate it in the water to loosen any grit. Let stand for a few minutes. Lift out the escarole and transfer it to another bowl, leaving any grit in the bottom of the bowl. Do not drain the escarole.

2. Heat the oil in a large skillet over medium heat. Add the pancetta and cook, stirring occasionally, until lightly browned, about 3 minutes. Stir in the garlic and cook until fragrant, about 1 minute.

3. Working in four or five additions, waiting for the first batch to wilt before adding more, add the escarole. Cover the skillet tightly and reduce the heat to medium-low. Cook, stirring occasionally, until the escarole is very tender, about 20 minutes. Season to taste with salt and pepper and serve hot.

Broccoli Rabe with Pancetta and Garlic

Substitute 1 pound broccoli rabe for the escarole. Cut the broccoli rabe crosswise into 1- to 2-inch pieces. Wash the broccoli rabe well, but do not dry it. In step 3, cook the broccoli rabe according to your taste, about 6 minutes for al dente, or 20 minutes for well-done and tender. The longer you cook the broccoli rabe, the less bitter and spicy it becomes, but it will never be as mild as broccoli.

mom's tomato pizza

MAKES 8 SERVINGS

Before you could buy a pizza on every corner, my sister Theresa and I would look forward to when Mom would make her special pie at home. Don't expect this to replicate the thin round pie at your neighborhood place. The dough (which is the same one used for American-style white sandwich bread) is pressed into jelly-roll pan and baked to make a thick and puffy rectangle topped with nothing more than crushed canned tomatoes. I suppose that you could add some shredded mozzarella and herbs if you like, but then it wouldn't be the same pie that we two young kids would eat in a single sitting.

DOUGH

¼ cup whole milk

¾ cup water

One ¼-ounce package active dry yeast (2¼ teaspoons)

2 tablespoons olive oil, plus more bowl, pan, and dough

1 tablespoon sugar

1 large egg yolk

1½ teaspoons fine table salt

3 cups unbleached all-purpose flour, plus more as needed

One 28- to 25-ounce can whole tomatoes in juice

1. Heat the milk in a small saucepan over medium heat until simmering. Remove from the heat and stir in the water. Pour the liquid into a small bowl and let it cool until warm (105° to 115°F, or like bath water). Sprinkle the yeast into the bowl and let stand until softened, about 5 minutes. Stir to dissolve the yeast.

2. Pour the yeast mixture into a large bowl. Stir in the oil, sugar, egg yolk, and salt. Gradually stir in enough of the flour to make a stiff dough that cannot be stirred. (To make it in an electric stand mixer, mix the yeast mixture, oil, sugar, yolk, and salt in the mixer bowl. Using the paddle attachment, with the mixer on low speed, gradually add enough flour, as necessary, to make a soft dough that cleans the sides of the bowl.)

3. Turn the dough out onto a floured work surface. Knead, adding more flour as necessary, to make a smooth, soft, and elastic dough, about 8 minutes. (Or change to the dough hook on the mixer. Knead, adding more flour as necessary, until the dough is smooth and elastic, about 8 minutes.)

4. Lightly oil a medium bowl. Shape the dough into a ball. Transfer the dough to the bowl and turn to coat with the oil. Turn the ball smooth side up and cover the bowl with plastic wrap. Let stand in a warm place until doubled in volume, about 1 hour. (The amount of sugar in this dough makes it rise quickly.)

(RECIPE CONTINUES)

5. Lightly oil a 10 by 15-inch jelly-roll pan with 1-inch sides. Punch down the dough and transfer to the pan. Pat and stretch the dough to fill the pan. If the dough springs back, cover it loosely with plastic wrap, let rest for 5 minutes, then stretch again. Cover with plastic wrap and let stand until the dough looks puffy and almost doubled in volume, 20 to 30 minutes.

6. Position a rack in the center of the oven and preheat the oven to 375°F.

7. Drain the tomatoes in a colander, discarding the juices. Coarsely crush the tomatoes with your hands. Spread the tomatoes over the dough, leaving a ½-inch border. Lightly brush the dough border with oil. Bake until the pizza bottom is golden brown (lift up the corner with a metal spatula to check), 25 to 30 minutes. Let cool slightly in the pan. Cut the pizza evenly into rectangles and serve hot.

frankie "boys"
with broccoli and cheese

MAKES 8 SERVINGS

Here's a vegetable version of my "Frankie boys" with fresh broccoli, Fontina, and Romano. When my guest list includes vegetarians, I serve this filling, as well as the sausage "boys" on page 122, to give a meatless choice, and sprinkle a little shredded Romano on the broccoli ones so they are easily identifiable. Even if you are a meat lover, this combination is irresistible.

FILLING

9 ounces broccoli (1 large stalk)

½ cup finely diced Fontina Val d'Aosta cheese (2 ounces)

⅔ cup finely grated Pecorino Romano cheese (1½ ounces)

3 tablespoons dried Italian-seasoned bread crumbs

3 tablespoons extra-virgin olive oil

½ teaspoon garlic powder

⅛ teaspoon hot red pepper flakes

1 recipe "Boys" Dough (page 122)

Olive oil, for brushing

2 tablespoons freshly grated Pecorino Romano cheese, for sprinkling

1. To make the filling: Trim the florets from the broccoli stem. Coarsely chop the stalk and pulse the pieces in a food processor until finely chopped. Transfer to a bowl. Repeat with the broccoli florets. (Or finely chop the broccoli by hand with a large knife.) You should have about 2 cups finely chopped broccoli. Add the Fontina, Romano, bread crumbs, extra-virgin olive oil, garlic powder, and red pepper flakes and stir together until the mixture is moistened.

2. Turn out the dough onto a work surface. Knead the dough briefly. Cut the dough into 8 equal portions, roll each into a ball, and cover loosely with plastic wrap. Working with one ball at a time, and keeping the remainder covered, flatten and roll out a ball into a 6-inch-diameter round. Spoon about ½ cup of the filling into the center of the round. Bring up the edges of the round to enclose the filling, and pinch the seams well closed. Turn the ball over and shape on the work surface between cupped hands into a round shape about 3½ inches in diameter. Arrange the "boys" on a large rimmed baking sheet, spacing them well apart. Loosely cover with plastic wrap and let stand in a warm place until they look somewhat puffed but not doubled, about 45 minutes.

3. Position a rack in the center of the oven and preheat the oven to 350°F.

4. Using kitchen scissors, snip a small slit in the top of each "boy." Lightly brush the tops with oil and sprinkle with the Romano cheese. Bake until the "boys" are golden brown, 30 to 35 minutes. Let cool on the baking sheet for 10 minutes. Serve warm or cooled to room temperature.

eggplant marinara

MAKES 8 SERVINGS

Eggplant marinara may look like eggplant Parmesan, but the difference is in the cheese, as this does not have any mozzarella. Eggplant soaks up oil like a sponge, but there are a couple of tricks to discourage this trait. Salting the eggplant before cooking helps, as does using a good amount of oil in the pan. We serve it as a side dish and as a vegetarian main course. Sometimes I'll make extra because warmed-up leftovers on a crusty roll makes a great hot sandwich.

2 large eggplants, about 1½ pounds each

Kosher salt

½ cup olive oil, plus more as needed

½ cup plus 2 tablespoons freshly grated Pecorino Romano cheese (about 2½ ounces)

1 recipe Red Wine Marinara Sauce (page 90)

1. Cut the eggplant into ⅔-inch rounds. Sprinkle the salt all over the eggplant and put the rounds in a colander. Let the eggplant drain in the kitchen sink for about 1 hour. Rinse well under cold running water and pat dry with kitchen towels.

2. Position a rack in the center of the oven and preheat the oven to 350°F. Lightly oil a 9 by 13-inch baking dish. Line a large rimmed baking sheet with paper towels and place it near the stove.

3. Heat the ½ cup of oil in a large skillet over medium-high heat until the oil is shimmering but not smoking. Working in batches, add the eggplant to the skillet and cook, turning once, until golden brown, about 5 minutes, adding more oil to the skillet as needed. Transfer the eggplant to the paper towels to drain, separating the layers with more paper towels.

4. Spread about ½ cup of the marinara sauce in the prepared baking dish. Top with one-third of the eggplant, one-third of the sauce, and ¼ cup of the Romano; repeat. Top with the remaining eggplant and sauce, and sprinkle with the remaining 2 tablespoons Romano.

5. Bake until the sauce is bubbling, about 30 minutes. Let stand for 5 minutes, then serve.

giambotta

MAKES 6 SERVINGS

Giambotta (pronounced, in Sicilian dialect, as "gee–am–bot") is just a vegetable stew. You can put whatever you want in it—some folks add potatoes to give it more bulk, and others include sweet bell peppers. You can eat it on its own with a hunk of bread for a meal, or put it on top of pasta as a sauce. It is as good hot as it is cold. About the only thing it isn't good for is dessert!

6 tablespoons olive oil, plus more as needed

2 medium zucchini, cut into ½-inch half-moons

1 medium yellow onion, chopped

2 garlic cloves, finely chopped

1 small eggplant, about 1 pound, cut into 1-inch cubes

One 28-ounce can plum tomatoes in juice, coarsely chopped, juices reserved

½ cup water

6 ounces green beans, cut into 1-inch lengths

1 teaspoon dried oregano

½ teaspoon hot red pepper flakes

Kosher salt

1. Heat the 2 tablespoons of the oil in a large heavy-bottomed saucepan over medium-high heat. Add the zucchini and cook, stirring occasionally, until beginning to brown, about 5 minutes. Stir in the onion and garlic and cook, stirring occasionally, until the onion has softened, about 3 minutes. Transfer the mixture to a medium bowl. Wipe out the saucepan with paper towels to remove any bits of vegetable.

2. Add the remaining 4 tablespoons oil to the saucepan and heat over medium-high heat until shimmering but not smoking. Add the eggplant and cook, stirring occasionally, until lightly browned, about 5 minutes. Return the onion mixture to the saucepan. Stir in the tomatoes with their juices and the water. Add the green beans, oregano, and red pepper flakes and stir to combine. Bring to a boil, then reduce the heat to medium-low. Cover the saucepan and cook, stirring occasionally, until the vegetables are tender and the sauce has thickened, about 30 minutes. Season to taste with salt. Serve the giambotta hot, warm, or cooled to room temperature.

roasted fennel
with parmesan and pine nuts

MAKES 6 SERVINGS

Usually when I am cooking, I concentrate my efforts on the main course, and like to make simple side dishes. Here is one that can't be much easier. I hear people say that fennel tastes like licorice, but in this dish, roasting makes it sweet and Parmesan gives it a savory flavor. Try this terrific side dish with grilled pork chops or sausages.

2 medium fennel bulbs, about 14 ounces each, top stalks and fronds removed

2 tablespoons olive oil, plus more for the baking dish

Kosher salt and freshly ground black pepper

½ cup freshly grated Parmesan cheese

¼ cup pine nuts

1 lemon cut in wedges

1. Position a rack in the center of the oven and preheat the oven to 400°F. Lightly oil a 9 by 13-inch baking dish.

2. Cut each fennel bulb lengthwise into ½-inch slabs. Place in the prepared baking dish and drizzle with the 2 tablespoons oil. Toss the fennel to coat, and arrange, overlapping as necessary, in the dish. Add about 2 tablespoons of water to the dish, and lightly season the fennel to taste with the salt (the Parmesan will be salty) and pepper. Cover tightly with aluminum foil.

3. Bake for 30 minutes. Sprinkle the Parmesan over the fennel. Continue baking until the fennel is tender when pierced with the tip of a small, sharp knife and the Parmesan is golden brown, about 30 minutes more.

4. Toast the pine nuts in a small skillet over medium heat, stirring occasionally, until toasted, about 3 minutes. Transfer the pine nuts to a plate and let them cool.

5. Sprinkle the pine nuts over the fennel. Transfer to a bowl and serve hot, with the lemon wedges for squeezing the juice over the fennel.

green beans
with red potatoes

Crisp vegetables can be good, but so can vegetables that have been cooked until they are very tender, just like these green beans paired with potatoes in a tomato sauce. All of the flavors mix together to become a fantastic side dish for simply prepared meats and seafood.

....

3 tablespoons olive oil

1 pound red-skinned potatoes, scrubbed but unpeeled, cut into ½-inch wedges

1 medium yellow onion, finely chopped

2 garlic cloves, minced

1 cup water

½ cup dry sherry

2 tablespoons tomato paste

1 teaspoon dried oregano

8 ounces green beans, cut into 1-inch pieces

½ teaspoon kosher salt, plus more as needed

¼ teaspoon freshly ground black pepper, plus more as needed

3 tablespoons freshly grated Parmesan cheese

1. Heat the oil in a large skillet over medium-high heat until it is very hot but not smoking. Add the potatoes, cut sides down, and cook, turning once, until golden brown on both sides but not tender, about 6 minutes. Using a slotted spoon, transfer the potatoes to a serving bowl, leaving the oil in the skillet.

2. Add the onion and garlic to the skillet and reduce the heat to medium. Cook, stirring occasionally, until the onion has softened, about 3 minutes. Add the water, sherry, tomato paste, and oregano and stir to dissolve the tomato paste. Return the potatoes to the skillet and scatter the green beans on top. Season with the ½ teaspoon salt and ¼ teaspoon pepper. Bring to a boil. Reduce the heat to medium-low and cover the skillet tightly. Simmer, stirring occasionally, until the potatoes are tender and the liquid has thickened, about 20 minutes. Season with additional salt and pepper as needed.

3. Transfer the potato mixture to a serving bowl. Sprinkle with the Parmesan cheese and serve hot.

annette's baked onions

I can still see my beloved friend, Annette Funicello, making these onions, which she would serve to go alongside just about any main course. They couldn't be easier to prepare, which is another reason why I still love them after all these years. And they look very appetizing, with the baked, caramelized onions falling open into a kind of flower shape. The salt is purposely left out because the bouillon cubes are salty. If you wish, substitute sweet onions for the red, or use a couple of each.

4 medium red onions, unpeeled, about 8 ounces each

2 tablespoons unsalted butter, cut into 4 slices

4 beef bouillon cubes

½ cup hot tap water

¼ teaspoon freshly ground black pepper

1. Position a rack in the center of the oven and preheat the oven to 400°F.

2. For each onion, trim the root end so the onion sits flat. Cut off a thin slice from the top. Cut the onion vertically into quarters, stopping just short of the bottom. Place the onions, root end down, in a 9 by 13-inch baking dish. Top each with a slice of butter and a bouillon cube, nestling the cube in the butter. Drizzle the hot water over the onions. Season with the pepper. Cover the dish with aluminum foil.

3. Bake for 1 hour. Discard the foil and baste the onions with the juices in the dish. Continue baking, basting occasionally, until the onions are beginning to brown and the juices have thickened, about 15 minutes more. Serve warm or cooled to room temperature, reminding the diners to remove the onion skins before eating.

roasted potatoes
with romano and rosemary

MAKES 6 SERVINGS

There are some main courses where the best side dish would be a few wedges of golden brown roasted potatoes. Too often the potatoes are undercooked, pale, and bland. I fix this by roasting them in a very hot oven and topping them with sharp Romano. Another tip: Use a big baking sheet (preferably a half-sheet pan measuring 17 by 13 inches) so the potatoes have plenty of space between them. If they are too close, they'll steam and not brown.

3 large baking potatoes, such as russets, about 12 ounces each

4 tablespoons olive oil

⅔ cup freshly grated Pecorino Romano cheese (about 1½ ounces)

1 teaspoon finely chopped fresh rosemary

Kosher salt and freshly ground black pepper

1. Position a rack in the center of the oven and preheat the oven to 425°F.

2. Scrub the potatoes under cold running water. You can peel them or leave the skins on. Cut each potato lengthwise into 8 wedges. Transfer the wedges to a large bowl and toss with 2 tablespoons of the oil to coat them.

3. Pour the remaining 2 tablespoons oil in a large baking sheet (preferably a half-sheet pan). Bake until the oil is very hot but not smoking, about 2 minutes. Remove from the oven. Spread the potatoes, flat sides down, on the hot baking sheet. Return to the oven and bake until the undersides are golden brown and release easily from the baking sheet with a metal spatula, about 25 minutes. Flip the potatoes and continue baking until the potatoes are crisp and golden brown.

4. Sprinkle the potatoes with the Romano and rosemary and toss well. Season to taste with salt and pepper. Transfer to a serving dish and serve hot.

mashed potatoes
with fontina and garlic

MAKES 6 SERVINGS

These are not your typical mashed potatoes, but jazzed up with Fontina cheese and lots of garlic. Don't let the amount of garlic put you off because it mellows when it is boiled with the potatoes. Fontina melts without getting stringy, so it is a good choice for this recipe. But you could use ½ cup (about 2 ounces) of crumbled Gorgonzola or freshly grated Parmesan or Romano.

3 pounds baking potatoes, such as russets, peeled and cut into 2-inch chunks

1 plump, large head garlic, broken into individual cloves, peeled

⅔ cup whole milk, heated to steaming

2 tablespoons unsalted butter, at room temperature

1 cup shredded Fontina cheese (4 ounces)

Kosher salt and freshly ground black pepper

1. Put the potatoes in a large saucepan and add enough cold salted water to cover by 2 inches. Bring to a boil over high heat. Add the garlic. Reduce the heat to medium-low and cook until the potatoes are tender when pierced with the tip of a small, sharp knife, 20 to 25 minutes. Drain well.

2. Return the potatoes to their cooking pot. Cook over low heat, stirring often, until they begin to film the bottom of the saucepan, about 2 minutes. Remove from the heat. Mash with a handheld masher or whip with an electric hand mixer, adding the milk and butter. Beat in the Fontina. Season to taste with salt and pepper. Serve hot.

radicchio
with ricotta and prosciutto stuffing

MAKES 10 ROLLS

Red-purple radicchio usually shows up in salads. But the leaves of this nice-looking vegetable can also be rolled, stuffed, and baked to make a side dish for a special occasion—maybe to go with a holiday roast. Truthfully, this is so good that you might just want to serve it as a supper or lunch main course. Leftovers heat up beautifully, so make the rolls ahead, if you wish.

Olive oil, for the baking dish and drizzling.

1 large head radicchio, about 10 ounces

FILLING

1 cup fresh ricotta cheese (4 ounces), drained

⅔ cup freshly grated Pecorino Romano cheese (about 1½ ounces)

⅔ cup diced prosciutto

¼ cup plain dried bread crumbs (see page 8)

2 scallions, white and pale green parts, finely chopped

1 garlic clove, minced

Freshly ground black pepper

1 large egg yolk

1. Position a rack in the center of the oven and preheat the oven to 350°F. Lightly oil a 9 by 13-inch baking dish. Bring a large saucepan of water to a boil over high heat.

2. To prepare the radicchio: Using a small knife, cut out the radicchio core. Separate the head into individual leaves, saving the very small inner leaves for another use (such as salad). Add the radicchio to the boiling water and cook just until they are pliable, about 30 seconds. Drain in a colander, rinse with cold running water, and drain well. Pat the leaves dry with paper towels.

3. To make the filling: Stir the ricotta, Pecorino Romano, prosciutto, bread crumbs, scallions, and garlic together. Season to taste with the pepper. Stir in the egg yolk.

4. For each roll, spoon about 3 tablespoons of the filling into the center of a large leave (or overlap two smaller leaves together, if necessary). Fold in the right and left sides and roll up into a thick cylinder. Place, seam side down, in the baking dish. (At this point, the radicchio can be covered with plastic wrap and refrigerated for up to 4 hours before baking.) Drizzle the stuffed radicchio with oil.

5. Bake until the radicchio rolls are lightly browned, about 30 minutes. Let cool for 5 minutes and serve.

desserts

CANNOLI-RUM LAYER CAKE 186

LIMONCELLO POUND CAKE 189

BANANA AND GRAHAM CRACKER ICEBOX CAKE 190

ITALIAN RICOTTA CHEESECAKE 192

STRUFFOLI 195

CHOCOLATE SPICE COOKIES 196

BUTTER TWISTS 198

SPRITZ COOKIES 200

ITALIAN PUFFED COOKIES 201

RAINBOW COOKIES 202

RICOTTA FRITTERS WITH FRESH BERRIES 205

cannoli-rum layer cake

MAKES 10 SERVINGS

Every Italian American loves cannoli—the crisp tubes of fried pastry filled with sweet ricotta. The pastry is not easy to make at home, which is why we usually buy our cannoli at bakeries. Instead, we use the ricotta cream to fill layers of Mom's sponge cake. Mom's cake is made with oil, which is a great trick because butter-based cakes get hard when refrigerated, and this dessert should be served chilled.

CAKE

Softened butter and flour, for the pans

¾ cup whole milk

½ cup vegetable oil

2 teaspoons vanilla extract

2 cups all-purpose flour

1 tablespoon baking powder

1 teaspoon fine table salt

7 large eggs, at room temperature

1½ cups granulated sugar

1 teaspoon cream of tartar

FILLING

1 cup heavy cream

½ cup confectioners' sugar

1 teaspoon vanilla extract

1 pound fresh ricotta cheese, drained (see page 6)

1 cup mini chocolate chips

WHIPPED CREAM

1½ cups heavy cream

3 tablespoons confectioners' sugar

1½ teaspoons vanilla extract

8 tablespoons golden or amber rum

10 large strawberries

1. To make the cake: Position a rack in the center of the oven and preheat the oven to 350°F. Lightly butter the insides of two 9-inch round by 2-inch deep cake pans. Line the bottoms with wax or parchment paper rounds. Dust the sides with flour and tap out the excess.

2. Heat the milk in a small saucepan over medium heat until tiny bubbles form around the edges. Remove from the heat. Stir in the oil and vanilla and let cool until warm.

3. Whisk the flour, baking powder, and salt together in a medium bowl. Beat the egg yolks in a large bowl with a handheld electric mixer on high speed until they begin to thicken. (Or whisk them by hand.) Gradually add the granulated sugar and continue beating (or whisking) until the mixture is pale and thickened, about 3 minutes (or 5 minutes by hand). With the mixer on low speed, add the flour mixture in thirds, alternating with two equal additions of the warm milk mixture, beating until smooth after each addition, and scraping down the sides of the bowl as needed with a rubber spatula.

4. Using clean beaters (or a clean whisk), whip the egg whites in a large clean bowl until foamy. Add the cream of tartar and continue whipping until the whites form stiff, shiny peaks. Stir about one-quarter of the whites into the batter to lighten it, then fold in the remainder. Divide the batter evenly between the cake pans and smooth the tops.

5. Bake until the cakes are golden and spring when gently pressed in the centers, about 30 minutes. Let cool in the pans on wire cake racks for 5 minutes. Run a knife around the inside edge of each pan and invert and unmold the cakes onto the racks. Peel off the wax paper. Turn the cakes right side up and let cool completely.

6. To make the filling: Whip the heavy cream, confectioners' sugar, and vanilla in a chilled medium bowl with an electric mixer until the cream is stiff. Add the ricotta and whisk together just until the mixture is smooth. Fold in the mini chocolate chips.

7. To make the whipped cream: Whip the heavy cream, confectioners' sugar, and vanilla in a chilled medium bowl with an electric mixer until the cream is stiff. Transfer about ¾ cup of the whipped cream to a pastry bag fitted with a ½-inch star pastry tip.

8. Using a long serrated knife, cut each cake layer in half horizontally. Place a cake layer on a serving platter and slip strips of wax paper underneath it to protect the platter from the cream. Brush the cake layer with 2 tablespoons of the rum. Spread with one-third of the filling. Repeat with the remaining cake layers, rum, and filling, ending with a cake layer and rum. Spread the top and sides of the cake with the remaining whipped cream. Pipe 10 large rosettes around the perimeter of the top of the cake, and place a strawberry on each rosette. Refrigerate the cake, uncovered, for at least 1 hour and up to 1 day. Slice and serve.

limoncello pound cake

MAKES 12 SERVINGS

It's good to have a good old-fashioned pound cake on hand for snacking, Mom's recipe follows that tradition, but lately I've gussied it up a bit with a soaking of limoncello. (I recommend storing a bottle of this Italian lemon liqueur in the freezer to have ready to serve as an after-dinner treat.) Plain or fancy, this cake is good either way. And it also makes a great shortcake with fresh berries and whipped cream, particularly with the lemon flavor from the liqueur.

Softened butter and flour, for the cake pan

4 cups all-purpose flour

1 tablespoon plus 1 teaspoon baking powder

½ teaspoon fine table salt

1 cup limoncello

¾ cup whole milk

1 cup (2 sticks) unsalted butter, at room temperature

3 cups sugar

8 large eggs, at room temperature

1 teaspoon vanilla extract

Finely grated zest of 1 lemon

1. Position a rack in the center of the oven and preheat the oven to 350°F. Lightly butter the inside of a 12-cup tube pan with a removable bottom, such as angel food cake pan. Dust the inside with flour and tap out the excess.

2. Whisk the flour, baking powder, and salt together in a medium bowl. Combine ¼ cup of the limoncello with the milk. Beat the butter in a large bowl with an electric mixer on high speed until creamy. Gradually beat in the sugar and continue beating until the mixture is light in color and texture, about 3 minutes. (Or cream the butter and sugar well by hand.) With the mixer on low speed, add (or stir in by hand) the eggs, one at a time, beating well after each addition. Mix in the vanilla and lemon zest. Add the flour in thirds, alternating with two equal additions of milk, beating until smooth after each addition and scraping down the sides of the bowl as needed. Scrape the batter into the cake pan and smooth the top.

3. Bake until the cake is golden brown and a long bamboo skewer inserted into the center comes out clean, about 1¼ hours. Transfer to a wire cake rack and let cool in the pan for 10 minutes.

4. Run a knife around the inside edges of the pan and the tube. Invert the cake onto the rack and place the rack over a rimmed baking sheet. Pierce the upturned bottom of the cake all over with the bamboo skewer in a few places, and brush half of the remaining ¾ cup limoncello over the warm cake. Let the cake cool for 10 to 15 minutes. Turn the cake right side up, pierce the top all over with the skewer, and brush with the remaining limoncello. Let the cake cool completely. (The cake can be covered with plastic wrap and stored at room temperature for up to 3 days.) Slice and serve.

banana and graham cracker icebox cake

MAKES 9 TO 12 SERVINGS

While I was gathering the recipes for this book, I had a craving for my absolute favorite of Mom's desserts, layered banana and graham cracker pudding. It was not beautiful or fancy, but every bite was cool and sweet, and I hadn't had it in decades. I called my sister Theresa and got the recipe, but not before she insisted, "And you must use *homemade* vanilla pudding and *real* whipped cream!" So, when I bought the graham crackers, guess what? The recipe was on the back of the box! Was it with homemade pudding and real whipped cream? No way! (But I will let you buy the caramel sauce if you don't feel like making it.)

VANILLA PUDDING

1 cup granulated sugar

¼ cup cornstarch

4 cups whole milk

4 large eggs

4 tablespoons (½ stick) unsalted butter

2 teaspoons vanilla extract

WHIPPED CREAM

1 cup heavy cream

2 tablespoons confectioners' sugar

½ teaspoon vanilla extract

4 ripe bananas, peeled and cut into thin rounds

16 to 18 whole graham crackers

CARAMEL SAUCE

1 cup granulated sugar

¼ cup water

1 tablespoon light corn syrup

½ cup heavy cream, heated to steaming

2 tablespoons unsalted butter

1 teaspoon vanilla extract

Pinch of fine table salt

1. To make the vanilla pudding: Whisk the granulated sugar and cornstarch together well in a medium heavy-bottomed saucepan. Gradually whisk in the milk. Cook over medium heat, whisking constantly, until simmering and thickened, about 5 minutes. Remove from the heat.

2. Whisk the eggs together in a heatproof medium bowl. Gradually whisk in about half of the hot milk mixture. Return this mixture to the mixture in the saucepan. Cook over medium-low heat, whisking constantly, until the pudding comes to a full boil, then cook, still whisking, for 30 seconds more. Remove from the heat. Add the butter and vanilla and whisk until the butter has melted. Strain the pudding through a fine-mesh wire sieve into a heatproof medium bowl. Cover the pudding with plastic wrap, pressing the wrap directly onto the surface. (This prevents a skin from forming.) Pierce a few slits in the wrap with the tip of a small knife, and let cool until tepid, about 1 hour. (You can speed this up by putting the bowl in a larger bowl of iced water for about 20 minutes.)

3. To make the whipped cream: Whip the cream, confectioners' sugar, and vanilla together in a chilled medium bowl with an electric mixer on high speed until the cream forms stiff peaks.

4. To assemble the pudding: Place one-third of the graham crackers, breaking them to fit, into the bottom of a 9 by 13-inch baking dish. Spread with one-third of the pudding and top with one-third of the bananas. Repeat twice, finishing with the bananas. Spread the whipped cream over the pudding, covering

the bananas completely. Refrigerate, uncovered, for at least 4 hours or up to 1 day; the longer the better.

5. To make the caramel sauce: Combine the granulated sugar, water, and corn syrup in a medium heavy-bottomed saucepan. Cook over high heat, stirring constantly, until boiling. Stop stirring and cook, washing down the crystals that form on the sides of the saucepan with a bristle brush dipped in water, until the caramel is the color of an old penny and smoking lightly, about 5 minutes. Reduce the heat to very low. Slowly and carefully stir in the hot cream (it will bubble up) and stir until the caramel is dissolved and the sauce is smooth. Remove from the heat and stir in the butter until dissolved. Let cool until warm. Stir in the vanilla and salt. Let cool completely. (The caramel sauce can be covered and refrigerated for up to 3 days.).

6. To serve, cut the chilled pudding into portions. Using a metal spatula, transfer each serving to a plate, whipped cream facing up. Drizzle with the caramel sauce and serve.

italian ricotta cheesecake

MAKES 8 TO 12 SERVINGS

For an Italian American, there is only one way to make cheesecake, and that is with ricotta. The cream cheese kind is okay, but it isn't Italian. And, as far as I'm concerned, it is worth getting fresh ricotta instead of the standard supermarket variety for this delicacy. The secret to this recipe is whipped cream folded into the batter. One tip: Don't plan on baking anything else for a couple of hours so the cheesecake can cool completely in the turned-off oven.

1 tablespoon unsalted butter, softened

2 tablespoons graham cracker crumbs

2 pounds fresh ricotta cheese, drained

1⅔ cups sugar

5 large eggs, separated, at room temperature

⅔ cup all-purpose flour, sifted

Finely grated zest of 1 lemon

1 teaspoon vanilla extract

⅔ cup heavy cream

1. Position a rack in the center of the oven and preheat the oven to 425°F. Grease the inside of an 8-inch round by 3-inch deep springform pan with the softened butter. Sprinkle in the graham cracker crumbs and coat the bottom of the pan with the crumbs, leaving the excess on the bottom of the pan.

2. While beating the ricotta in a large bowl with an electric mixer on medium speed (or whisking by hand), gradually add ⅔ cup of the sugar. Beat (or whisk) in the yolks, one at a time, followed by the flour, lemon zest, and vanilla. Using clean beaters (or a clean whisk), whip the egg whites in a separate clean bowl until soft peaks form. Gradually whip in the remaining ⅔ cup sugar and continue whipping until stiff, shiny peaks form. Fold the mixture into the batter, just until almost combined.

3. Whip the cream in a chilled medium bowl until stiff. Add to the batter and fold in until smooth. Spread the batter in the pan and smooth the top.

4. Bake for 20 minutes. Reduce the heat to 350°F and continue baking until the sides of the cheesecake are puffed and lightly browned, about 35 minutes more. Turn off the oven and prop the door ajar with a wooden spoon. Let the cheesecake cool completely in the oven, at least 2 hours.

5. Run a knife around the inside edges of the cheesecake and remove the sides of the pan. Cover the cheesecake with plastic wrap and refrigerate until chilled, at least 4 hours or up to 3 days. Slice and serve.

struffoli

Struffoli is another heritage recipe that almost every Italian American family serves at Christmas—tiny fried balls of dough shaped into a wreath and held together with a honey syrup. Some families put some baking powder in the dough, but this version leaves it out so the fried bits stay crisper. This is best served the day you make it.

1½ cups unbleached all-purpose flour

¼ teaspoon fine table salt

3 large eggs, at room temperature, beaten together

1 teaspoon vanilla extract

Vegetable oil, for deep-frying and coating the spoons

Softened butter, for the platter

¾ cup honey

2 tablespoons sugar

Multicolored sprinkles (nonpareils), for decoration

Note: The struffoli can be stored at room temperature, uncovered, for up to 12 hours.)

1. Whisk the flour and salt together in a medium bowl. Make a well in the center and add the eggs and vanilla. Stir to make a soft dough. Shape the dough into a ball and wrap in plastic wrap. Let stand at room temperature for about 30 minutes.

2. Line 2 baking sheets with wax or parchment paper. Cut the dough into sixths. Keeping the remaining dough covered, on a lightly floured work surface, and working with one-sixth at a time, roll the dough underneath your hands, moving your hands apart in a horizontal movement while rolling, until the dough is rolled and stretched into a long rope about ½ inch wide. Using a sharp knife, cut the dough into ½-inch-long pieces. Do not bother to roll these into balls, as they will puff when fried. Transfer the dough pieces to the baking sheets, separating the pieces so they don't stick together. Let stand to slightly dry the dough pieces, about 15 minutes.

3. Line a large roasting pan with crumpled paper towels. Pour enough oil into a large, deep saucepan to come 3 inches up the sides and heat over high heat until it registers 350°F on a deep-frying thermometer. Working in batches without crowding, carefully transfer the dough to the oil and deep-fry until golden brown, about 2 minutes. Using a wire spider or slotted spoon, transfer the fried dough to the paper towels in the roasting pan. Repeat with the remaining dough, separating the layers with more paper towels.

4. Lightly butter a round serving platter. Lightly oil 2 metal spoons. In a saucepan large enough to hold all of the dough pieces, bring the honey and sugar to a boil over high heat, stirring often to dissolve the sugar. Boil for 30 seconds. Add all of the dough pieces at once and stir gently until they are covered with the syrup. Pour the struffoli out onto the platter. Using the oiled spoons, shape the mound into a wreath. Decorate with a shower of sprinkles. Let cool completely.

chocolate spice cookies

MAKES ABOUT 5 DOZEN

This is a chocolate contribution to the Christmas cookie lineup, with a little bit of spice to give them an unexpected flavor that goes really well with an after-dinner cup of coffee. Actually, they taste a lot like little chocolate cakes—and who doesn't love chocolate cake? Because they are so easy to make, this recipe is a good one to have when you need a lot of cookies in a relatively short time.

COOKIES

1 cup (2 sticks) unsalted butter, at room temperature

⅔ cup granulated sugar

2 large eggs, at room temperature

1 teaspoon vanilla extract

4 cups all-purpose flour

⅔ cup natural cocoa powder

2 tablespoons baking powder

¼ teaspoon ground cinnamon

½ teaspoon ground cloves

½ teaspoon fine table salt

1 cup whole milk

1½ cups coarsely chopped walnuts or pecans (6 ounces)

CLASSIC COOKIE ICING

3¼ cups (1 pound) confectioners' sugar

½ cup whole milk, plus more as needed

1 teaspoon light corn syrup

Chocolate jimmies (sprinkles), for decorating (optional)

1. To make the cookies: Cream the butter in bowl of a stand electric mixer fitted with the paddle attachment on high speed (or in a large bowl with a wooden spoon) until creamy. Gradually beat in the sugar and mix until the mixture is light and fluffy, about 3 minutes. One at a time, beat in the eggs, beating well after each addition, followed by the vanilla.

2. Whisk the flour, cocoa, baking powder, cinnamon, cloves, and salt together in a medium bowl. With the mixer on low speed (or stirring by hand), add the flour mixture in thirds, alternating with two equal additions of the milk, and beating until smooth after each addition, scraping down the sides of the bowl as needed. Mix in the nuts. Cover and refrigerate the dough for about 30 minutes to chill slightly and make it easier to handle.

3. Position racks in the center and upper third of the oven and preheat the oven to 375°F. Line two large rimmed baking sheets with parchment paper.

4. Using a tablespoon for each cookie, roll the dough into balls. Place them about 1 inch apart on the prepared baking sheets. Bake, switching the position of the baking sheets from top to bottom and front to back halfway through the baking, until the cookies are very lightly browned on the bottoms, 12 to 15 minutes. Let the cookies cool for 3 minutes on the baking sheets, then transfer to wire cake racks to cool completely.

5. To make the icing: Sift the confectioners' sugar into a medium bowl. Add the milk and corn syrup and whisk until the icing is smooth; it should be a little thicker than heavy cream. Adjust the thickness, if necessary, with more milk, adding it a teaspoon at a time.

6. Place sheets of parchment or wax paper under the cookies on the racks. One at a time, hold each cookie by its edges, and dip, upside down, into the icing to coat its top. Shake off the excess icing. Return the cookie, right side up, to the wire rack. Let the icing set slightly, then sprinkle with the jimmies, if using. Let the icing set completely. Store the cookies in an airtight container, with the layers separated by parchment or wax paper, at room temperature, for up to 1 week.

butter twists

MAKES ABOUT 4 DOZEN

This recipe comes from the family of my good friend, John Peca, who I often turn to for great Italian food. These simple cookies are beauties, and although they may look difficult to make, it is easy to twist the dough into its distinctive spiral shape. In his family, they are just named biscotti, but since biscotti has come to be known as a specific kind of hard cookie, I now call these "twists."

1¼ cups (2½ sticks) unsalted butter, at room temperature

1 cup sugar

3 large eggs, plus 1 large egg yolk, beaten together, at room temperature

⅔ cup plus 1 tablespoon whole milk

1½ teaspoons vanilla extract

Finely grated zest of ½ lemon

5 cups all-purpose flour

¾ teaspoon fine table salt

2 tablespoons baking powder

Classic Cookie Icing (page 196)
Colored jimmies (sprinkles), for decorating (optional)

1. To make the cookies: Cream the butter in the bowl of a stand electric mixer fitted with the paddle attachment (or in a large bowl with a wooden spoon) on high speed until creamy. Gradually beat in the sugar and mix until the mixture is light and fluffy, about 3 minutes. Gradually beat in the egg mixture, beating well after each addition, followed by the vanilla and lemon zest.

2. Whisk the flour, baking powder, and salt together in another large bowl. With the mixer on low speed (or stirring by hand), add the flour mixture in thirds, alternating with two equal additions of the milk, and beating until smooth after each addition and scraping down the sides of the bowl as needed. Cover and refrigerate the dough for 1 hour to chill slightly and make it easier to handle.

3. Position racks in the center and upper third of the oven and preheat the oven to 375°F. Line two large rimmed baking sheets with parchment paper.

4. Using about 2 tablespoons for each, on a lightly floured work surface, roll the dough under your palms into a rope about 7 inches long. Bend the rope into a U shape. Holding the ends of the U together, twist the dough two or three times to get a spiral shape. Transfer the twist to the lined baking sheets, spacing them about 1½ inches apart.

5. Bake, switching the position of the baking sheets from top to bottom and front to back halfway through the baking, until the cookies are lightly browned on the bottoms, 12 to 15 minutes. Let the cookies cool for 3 minutes on the baking sheets, then transfer to wire cake racks to cool completely.

6. Place sheets of parchment or wax paper under the cookies on the racks. One at a time, hold each cookie by its edges, and dip, upside down, into the icing to coat its top. Shake off the excess icing. Return the cookie, right side up, to the wire rack. Let the icing set slightly, then sprinkle with the jimmies, if using. Let the icing set completely. Store the cookies in an airtight container, with the layers separated by parchment or wax paper, at room temperature, for up to 1 week.

spritz cookies

For an Italian American mom, a cookie press is an essential kitchen tool. She might only use it once a year to make Christmas cookies, but then it gets a workout. The bakery is rare that sells cookies this buttery and crisp. If you don't already have one, cookie presses are inexpensive and easy to find online and in kitchen shops.

1 cup (2 sticks) unsalted butter, at cool room temperature

¾ cup sugar

1 large egg, at room temperature

1 teaspoon vanilla or lemon extract, or ½ teaspoon of each extract

2¼ cups unbleached all-purpose flour

36 candied cherries, cut into halves, as needed

Special Equipment: A cookie press and 5-point disk

1. Position a rack in the top third and center of the oven and pre-heat the oven to 350°F. Have ready 2 large *ungreased* rimmed baking sheets.

2. Beat the butter the bowl of an electric stand mixer fitted with the paddle attachment at high speed (or in a large bowl with a wooden spoon) until the butter is smooth, about 1 minute. Gradually beat in the sugar and continue beating until the mixture is light in color and texture, about 3 minutes more. Beat in the egg and vanilla. With the mixer on low speed, mix (or stir in) in the flour to make a soft dough.

3. Fit a cookie press with a 5-point disk. Working in batches, transfer the dough to the press. Pipe the dough onto the ungreased baking sheets, spacing the cookies 1 inch apart. (The dough will not adhere to greased sheets or ones that have been lined with parchment paper or silicone mats.) Place a candied cherry half into the center of each cookie.

4. Bake, switching the positions of the baking sheets from top to bottom and front to back halfway through the baking, until the cookies are barely beginning to brown around the edges, about 12 minutes. Let cool on the baking sheets for 3 minutes. Transfer to wire cake racks to cool completely. Wash, dry, and cool the baking sheets before piping out the remaining cookies. (The cookies can be stored in an airtight container for up to 5 days.)

italian puffed cookies

MAKES ABOUT 5 DOZEN

I found this simple drop cookie in Mom's recipe book and it has the usual basic flavorings of butter, sugar, and vanilla. If you like, add 1 teaspoon coarsely ground anise seed to spice them up. It's easiest to beat the eggs and sugar (the key to their puffiness) with a hand mixer, because the mixture is too small to whip up in a large stand mixer.

4 tablespoons (½ stick) unsalted butter

3 large eggs, at room temperature

½ cup sugar

2¼ cups all-purpose flour

1 tablespoon plus 1 teaspoon baking powder

½ teaspoon fine table salt

Classic Cookie Icing (page 196)

Nonpareils (colored sugar balls), for decorating

1. Position racks in the center and top third of the oven and preheat the oven to 325°F. Line two large rimmed baking sheets with parchment paper.

2. Melt the butter in a small saucepan over low heat. Remove from the heat and let cool to tepid.

3. Beat the eggs and sugar together in a large bowl with a hand-held electric mixer on high speed until the mixture is thickened and pale yellow, about 3 minutes. (Or whisk with a large balloon whisk for about 5 minutes.) Mix in the cooled butter.

4. Whisk the flour, baking powder, and salt together in a medium bowl to combine. Gradually stir the flour mixture into the beaten egg mixture to make a sticky dough.

5. Drop the dough by tablespoons onto the lined baking sheets, spacing the mounds about 1 inch apart. Bake, switching the position of the baking sheets from top to bottom and front to back halfway through the baking, until the cookies are lightly browned, about 15 minutes. Let cool on the baking sheets for 3 minutes, then transfer to wire cake racks to cool completely.

6. Place sheets of parchment or wax paper under the cookies on the racks. One at a time, hold each cookie by its edges, and dip, upside down, into the icing to coat its top. Shake off the excess icing. Return the cookie, right side up, to the wire rack. Let the icing set slightly, then sprinkle with the nonpareils. Let the icing set completely. Store the cookies in an airtight container, with the layers separated by parchment or wax paper, at room temperature, for up to 1 week.

rainbow cookies

Red, green, and yellow strips of cake, topped with chocolate, these cookies are a staple at Italian American bakeries, even though they are not sold in Italy itself. They are also known as Neapolitans, Venetians, or Seven-Layer Cookies. The instructions look long, but these are not difficult to make at home and you will get a lot of gorgeous cookies for your efforts. You bake three layers for stacking, and this job goes quickly with three identical foil cake pans, easily purchased at supermarkets.

....

Softened butter and flour, for the pans

One 8-ounce can or 7-ounce tube almond paste (see Note), coarsely chopped

1 cup sugar

1 cup (2 sticks) unsalted butter, at room temperature

4 large eggs, separated

½ teaspoon almond extract

2 cups unbleached all-purpose flour

Green, red, and yellow food coloring, preferably paste

One 12-ounce jar apricot or raspberry preserves

2 tablespoons golden rum or water

¼ cup heavy cream

4 ounces semisweet chocolate, coarsely chopped

1. Position racks in the center and top third of the oven and preheat the oven to 350°F. Lightly butter three 9 by 12-inch disposable aluminum foil cake pans. Line the bottoms of the pans with parchment or wax paper. Dust the sides of the pans with flour, and tap out the excess flour.

2. Process the almond paste and sugar together in a food processor fitted with the metal chopping blade until the almond paste is completely pulverized, about 1 minute. (Or do this in batches in a blender.) Pour the mixture into a large bowl. Add the butter and beat with an electric mixer on high speed until light in color and texture, about 2 minutes. One at a time, beat in the egg yolks, beating well after each addition, then the almond extract. Gradually beat in the flour.

3. Using clean beaters, whip the egg whites in a clean, medium bowl until soft peaks form. Stir about one-quarter of the beaten whites into the almond paste mixture to lighten it. Fold in the remaining whites.

4. Divide the batter into thirds, placing one portion in each of three bowls. Tint each separately with green, red, and yellow food coloring. Spread each evenly in a baking pan.

5. Bake until the cakes are firm when pressed in the centers with a finger and the edges are very lightly browned, about 12 minutes. (The layers will be about ¼ inch high.) Transfer the cakes in their pans to wire cake racks and let cool for 10 minutes. Invert the cakes onto the racks and remove the paper. Let cool completely.

(RECIPE CONTINUES)

6. Bring the preserves and rum to a boil in a small saucepan over medium heat. Cook, stirring often, until the mixture has thickened slightly, about 2 minutes. Rub through a wire strainer set over a bowl; discard the solids in the strainer.

7. Place the yellow layer, smooth side up, on a cutting board. Spread with half of the preserves. Top with the red layer, smooth side up, and spread with the remaining preserves. Top with the green layer, smooth side up. Place another cutting board on top to weight the stacked cake layers. Let stand until the preserves are set, about 2 hours.

8. Bring the heavy cream to a simmer in a small saucepan over medium heat. Remove from the heat. Add the chocolate and let stand until the chocolate softens, about 3 minutes. Stir until smooth and melted.

9. Using a sharp thin knife, trim the edges from the stacked cake layers to make a rectangle with smooth edges. Transfer the stacked cake layers to a wire cake rack set over a rimmed baking sheet. Pour the chocolate mixture over the top of the stacked cake layers. Spread evenly with a metal cake spatula. Let stand until the chocolate is cooled at set, about 2 hours (or refrigerate for 1 hour.)

10. Slide the pastry onto a work surface. Using a sharp thin knife, cut horizontally into 9 equal strips, then vertically into 9 equal pieces per strip to make 81 rectangles. Separate the cookies. (The cookies can be stored, refrigerated first to harden the chocolate topping, in an airtight container, separated by sheets of wax paper, for up to 1 week.)

Note: Almond paste, made from ground almonds and sugar, is available canned or in foil-wrapped tubes at most supermarkets and at specialty food shops While there is a 1-ounce difference in the package weights, the discrepancy doesn't make any difference. Do not confuse almond paste with marzipan, which is prepared with ground almonds and syrup. Marzipan has a softer consistency and sweeter flavor that is more appropriate for candy-making than baking.

ricotta fritters
with fresh berries

With ricotta on hand in the refrigerator, it only takes a few steps to prepare these hot, creamy morsels to serve with seasonal berries. Because they are fried, the fritters are a special treat, so the fresh fruit makes them seem a bit less sinful.

FRITTERS

8 ounces (1 cup) fresh ricotta cheese, drained

½ cup all-purpose flour

⅔ cup plus 1 tablespoon granulated sugar

2 large eggs, beaten

¼ teaspoon baking powder

Pinch of fine table salt

Vegetable oil, for deep-frying

Confectioners' sugar, for serving

12 ounces to 1 pound fresh berries, such as blueberries, blackberries, raspberries, and sliced strawberries, in any combination (about 3 cups)

1. Position a rack in the center of the oven and preheat the oven to 200°F. Line a large rimmed baking sheet with paper towels.

2. To make the fritter batter: Put the ricotta cheese in a medium bowl. Sift in the flour, and add the granulated sugar, eggs, baking powder, and salt. Stir well until combined. Set the batter aside while heating the oil.

3. Pour enough oil into a large saucepan to come about 2 inches up the sides and heat over high heat until it reaches 350°F on a deep-frying thermometer. Working in batches without crowding, carefully add tablespoons of the batter into the oil. (It helps to use two dessertspoons, one to scoop up the fritter batter and the other to scrape it into the oil.) Deep-fry the fritters, turning them once, until golden brown. Using a slotted spoon, transfer the fritters to the paper towels and keep warm in the oven while frying the rest.

4. Sift confectioners' sugar over the fritters. For each serving, place two or three fritters on a dessert plate, and add a spoonful of the berries. Serve immediately.

acknowledgments

First of all, I would like to thank my friend, John Peca. Although he is a lawyer by profession, John is the best Italian cook I know, surpassing even many of the restaurant chefs who I have dined with over the years. He and his wife, Joanna, generously shared some of their family heritage recipes to exist in this book next to the ones from the Avallone's.

Also a longtime friend, Keith Frankel and I have worked together on various projects bringing good things into people's lives, and this book is a kind of culmination of those. Thanks, Keith, for your support and friendship over the years.

It is true to say that this book would not exist without my sister, Theresa, who has guarded Mom's recipe book over the decades. When we were kids eating pizza at the kitchen table in Philadelphia, we never would have thought that the recipe would end up in a book!

My gratitude to Philadelphia music world legend, "The Geator with the Heator," Jerry Blavat, for putting together a tour of our old haunts in South Philly, and for being a friend of over fifty years.

The people in my life that I love the most are also the people for whom I cook the most often. My wife, Kay; our children, Frank Junior, Tony, Dina, Laura, Joe, Nick, Kathryn, and Carla; and our grandchildren, Jonathan, Patrick, Kathryn, Connor, Nicole, Meghan, Mason, Bridget, Johnny, and Tucker.

Rick Rodgers, who I swear has supernatural powers because of the way he channeled my mom's recipes, cooked with me to create this book. Literary agent and artist's representative Alan Morel found a home for this book at St. Martin's Press, where editor BJ Berti held the reins to bring it to completion. Thanks also to our copy editor, Leah Stewart, and book designer, Jan Derevjanik.

index

31901056535240